Student Workbook

to accompany

FUNDAMENTALS OF STATISTICS FOR PSYCHOLOGY STUDENTS

Student Workbook
to accompany

FUNDAMENTALS OF STATISTICS FOR PSYCHOLOGY STUDENTS

James R. Misanin
Susquehanna University
Charles F. Hinderliter
University of Pittsburgh at Johnstown

HarperCollinsPublishers

Student Workbook to accompany FUNDAMENTALS OF STATISTICS FOR PSYCHOLOGY STUDENTS

ISBN:0-673-46526-8
91 92 93 94 95 9 8 7 6 5 4 3 2 1

CONTENTS

Preface

PREFACE

To the Student:

The workbook, like the textbook, is written for the beginning psychology student who is taking a first course in statistics. The emphasis of the workbook is on mastering the language of statistics, applying statistical concepts, and on statistical reasoning and decision making. In each chapter of the workbook the section *Mastering the Language of Statistics* provides a fill-in-the-blank exercise that not only aids in your acquiring a statistical vocabulary but also serves as a detailed chapter summary to be used as a study guide. The true-false and the multiple-choice items appearing in this section also focus on vocabulary. Answers to all exercises in this section can be found in the *Key Terms and Definitions* section that immediately follows the *Detailed Textbook Outline* located at the beginning of each workbook chapter.

You should attempt to solve the workbook problems only after completing the textbook chapter. Solving the problems in the workbook should not only strengthen your statistical vocabulary, but also should help you identify problem areas or areas that require additional study that may not have been evident when working the *Progress Assessments* or *Review Exercises* in the textbook. At the very least, the workbook exercises, particularly those in the section on *Applying Statistical Concepts*, provide you with additional opportunities to apply what you have learned to the kinds of research or situations you are likely to encounter as a psychology student. Before the application exercises in the workbook, we provide an example application. The example application serves not only as a review of the textbook material but also provides you with the conceptual understanding and procedures necessary to complete the application exercises.

A section of *Meeting the Challenge of Statistics* is included in each workbook chapter to enhance your understanding of statistical reasoning and decision making. In Chapter 1 of the workbook we present a hypothetical experiment with an accompanying data set. In each chapter of the workbook we have you apply what you have learned in that chapter as well as the comparable textbook chapter to the hypothetical data set. In the textbook we advise and urge you to make your decisions about the statistical tests to use and the procedures to follow before collecting your data. The fact that you can apply to the hypothetical data set nearly all the procedures and tests that you encounter in the textbook and workbook should make it evident that a thorough understanding of statistics and statistical procedures is necessary for you to select beforehand the most appropriate method to analyze the data. This section should also make it clear that there is a variety of ways that data can be analyzed and interpreted.

Student Workbook to accompany

FUNDAMENTALS OF STATISTICS

FOR PSYCHOLOGY STUDENTS

CHAPTER 1
THE MEANING AND USE OF STATISTICS

DETAILED TEXTBOOK OUTLINE

Statistics Defined (Page 4)

Progress Assessment 1.1

Why Study Statistics (Page 4)

Progress Assessment 1.2

Two Functions of Statistics (Page 6)

Descriptive Statistics
Inferential Statistics
Progress Assessment 1.3

Defining Groups and Measures (Page 7)

Populations and Parameters
Samples and Statistics
Progress Assessment 1.4

Summary (Page 9)

Key Terms and Definitions (Page 9)

Review Exercises (Page 10)

Answers to Progress Assessments (Page 11)

KEY TERMS AND DEFINITIONS

descriptive statistics A branch of mathematics used to describe and summarize data.

finite population A population which has a limited number of members.

inferential statistics Statistics used to make accurate and efficient judgments about an entire group based upon the analysis of information obtained from a portion of the group.

infinite population A population that does not have a limit to the number of members.

N A symbol used to denote sample size.

numerical data Information collected as numbers.

parameters Measurements obtained from populations. Greek
    letters are used to symbolize parameters.

population All members of a group of people, places, objects,
    or events that share at least one common characteristic.

sample A subset, that is a portion, of a defined population.

sample statistics Usually referred to simply as statistics.
    Refers to measurements obtained from a sample. The symbols
    used to denote statistics are English letters.

statistics A term that can be used in any or all of the
    following ways (1) information collected as numbers, that
    is, numerical data; (2) measures obtained from samples; and
    (3) a branch of mathematics that deals with collecting,
    analyzing, and interpreting numerical data.

MASTERING THE LANGUAGE OF STATISTICS

Fill-in-the-Blanks

Write the appropriate term(s) in the space(s) provided.

The term "statistics" refers to _____ _____, that is,

information described and collected as numbers. The term

_____ also refers to measures of group characteristics.

The term is also used for the branch of mathematics that deals

with collecting, analyzing, and interpreting _____ ____.

Statistics that are used to describe a ____ ___, that is, a

collection of numerical information, are called _____

statistics. Descriptive statistics such as your classmates'

scores on their first statistics quiz serve merely to _____

a data set, whereas descriptive statistics such as the score

that most typifies the quiz scores or marks off the top 90

percent of the scores serve not only to describe a data set but

also to _____ it in such a way as to ascertain how your

classmates performed as a group. Thus, descriptive statistics are also used to _____ data efficiently.

Statistics that are used to make judgements about an entire group based upon the analysis of information obtained from a portion of the group are referred to as _____ statistics. The entire group about which the judgements are made is called a(n) _____. A(n) _____ consists of all members of a defined group that possess one or more specified characteristics. A(n)_____ population refers to a defined group that has a limited number of members, whereas a(n) _____ population refers to a group for which there is no limit to the number of members. Human beings is an example of a(n) _____ population. The stars in the universe is an example of a(n) _____ population. A measure of a population characteristic is called a(n) _____. Parameters are generally symbolized by _____ letters. A subset of a population is called a(n) _____. The size of a sample is designated by the letter ___ . Measurements obtained from a sample are referred to as _____ _____. Sample statistics are generally symbolized by _____ letters.

True-False Items

Place a T for true or an F for false in the space provided before each item.

1._____ The branch of mathematics used to summarize data is called summary statistics.

2._____ If a measure was obtained from all members of a group of people, places, objects, or events sharing a similar set of characteristics, it would be symbolized by a Greek letter.

3._____ The symbol N refers to the size of a sample statistic.

4.____ The term "statistics" refers to only numerical data.

5.____ A measure of a population characteristic is called a parameter.

6.____ The branch of mathematics used to make accurate and efficient judgements about an entire group based on the analysis of information collected from a sample or subset of the group is called descriptive statistics.

7.____ Numerical data refers to information collected from samples.

8.____ Measurements made on a sample are called statistics.

9.____ A group of objects sharing a common characteristic that does not have a limit to the number of its members is called an infinite population.

10.____ A report of the number of births on each day throughout the month of June at a particular hospital is an example of using statistics for inferential purposes.

11.____ The Scholastic Aptitude Test scores of students in your statistics class are compared to the test scores of all students at the university. All students at the university constitute the population and the students in your class are a sample from this population.

12.____ Albino rats of the Wistar strain (N = 25) were the subjects of an experiment on maternal behavior. The 25 rats constitute a sample.

Multiple-Choice Items

Blacken out the letter corresponding to the correct answer.

1. The average blood cholesterol level of a group of 80-year-old males selected from a number of nursing homes throughout the United States is an example of
   (a) numerical data.
   (b) descriptive statistics.
   (c) sample data.
   (d) all of the above.

2. The heights of all the first grade students in a particular elementary school are measured to determine the average height of the first grade class. This is an example of
   (a) using statistics to evaluate research.
   (b) using statistics for thinking and problem solving.
   (c) using statistics to complete research.
   (d) none of the above.

3. The first grade students referred to in problem 2 constitute
   (a) a sample.
   (b) a finite population.
   (c) an infinite population.
   (d) none of the above.

4. The average height of the first grade class referred to in problem 2 is an example of
   (a) a parameter.
   (b) inferential statistics.
   (c) a summary statistic.
   (d) descriptive statistics.

5. The heights of the individual first grade students referred to in problem 2 are _____, whereas the average height of the first grade students is a _____.
   (a) numerical data, a statistic
   (b) statistics, a parameter
   (c) parameters, numerical data
   (d) parameters, a statistic

6. A _____ is to a sample as a _____ is to a population.
   (a) parameter, statistic
   (b) parameter, parameter
   (c) statistic, statistic
   (d) statistic, parameter

7. Usually a Greek letter is used to symbolize
   (a) numerical data.
   (b) a statistic.
   (c) a parameter.
   (d) a sample characteristic.

8. All the planets in our solar system constitute
   (a) a sample of the planets in our solar system.
   (b) a sample of planets in the universe.
   (c) the finite population of planets in our solar system.
   (d) both b and c are correct.

9. The size of a sample is designated by
   (a) an English letter.
   (b) a statistic.
   (c) the symbol N.
   (d) all of the above.

10. The average size of all the planets in the universe would be
    (a) symbolized by a Greek Letter.
    (b) a parameter.
    (c) a statistic.
    (d) both a and b are correct.

11. The term "statistics" refers to
    (a) numerical data.
    (b) measures of sample characteristics.
    (c) a branch of mathematics.
    (d) all of the above.

12. Statistics that are used to make accurate and efficient
    judgments about a population are called
    (a) descriptive statistics.
    (b) inferential statistics.
    (c) summary statistics.
    (d) both a and b are correct.

APPLYING STATISTICAL CONCEPTS

Example Application

There are times when an individual's sensitivity to a particular
type of stimulus needs to be assessed. A doctor may need to
assess an individual's sensitivity to auditory stimuli if the
individual is complaining of hearing difficulties. Applicants
for an air traffic controller position may have their
sensitivity to visual stimuli displayed on a screen assessed.
In such cases, to judge the person's performance adequately the
rate (hit rate) at which the stimulus is claimed to be detected
when it is actually present must be compared with the rate
(false alarm rate) at which it is claimed to be detected when it
is not really present. Oftentimes these hit rates differ
depending on the instructions given. A psychology instructor is
interested in determining whether the hit and false alarm rates
for detecting auditory stimuli of students at the university who
are told not to say they detected the stimulus unless they were
absolutely sure will differ from the rates of students who are
told to say yes if there is the slightest possibility that the
stimulus is detected. The instructor has the sixty students in
a general psychology class serve as subjects in an experiment.
Half of the class was given one set of instructions and the
remaining half was given the other. The experimental trials
were presented and the instructor recorded the number of hits
and false alarms made by each student. He calculated the
average hit and false alarm rate for each set of instructions.
   If you can apply what you have learned in this chapter to
this experiment you know that the **numerical data**, the number of
hits and false alarms, were recorded for each member of two
samples (N = 30 each) from the **finite population** (students at
the university). The averages (**sample statistics**) of these data
sets not only serve to describe and summarize the data from the
two samples (**descriptive statistics**), but are also to be used by
the instructor to make judgments about the measures (**parameters**)
that would apply to the entire student body (**inferential
statistics**). The instructor is using statistics to **complete**

research and **solve the problem** about the effect of instructions on the students' perception of auditory stimuli.

Application Exercises

1. The term "dichotic" comes from the Greek root *dich* meaning "in two" and the adjective *otic* meaning "of or connected with the ear. "Dichotic listening refers to an experimental technique in which different auditory information is simultaneously presented to each ear of a subject. This experimental technique is sometimes used to study the influence of attention on short-term memory. Suppose in one such study fifty students are selected from the student body of a large university to be used as subjects in an experiment to determine to what extent short-term memory of auditory information depends upon paying attention to the information. Each of the students selected hears a different list of words in each ear and is instructed to repeat the words presented to one ear as they are being presented while disregarding those presented to the other ear. Immediately after the lists have been presented the student is read a list of words and asked how many of the words are recognized as familiar. This new list contains words from both lists. The average number of words from the unattended-to-list recognized as familiar is compared to the number of words from the attended-to-list recognized as familiar and is used to make a judgment about how inattention influences the short-term memory of students at the university.

   Determine

   a. the population of interest.

   b. whether the population is finite or infinite.

   c. whether the group on which the measures are taken constitute the population or a sample.

   d. if the measurements made on the group refer to statistics or parameters.

   e. which of the three ways statistics is referred to (for example, numerical data).

    f.   why statistics are being used (for example, evaluating research).

    g.   whether reference is to descriptive or inferential statistics, or both.

    h.   the numerical data.

    i.   the sample size (if appropriate).

    j.   the sample statistics mentioned (if appropriate).

2.   A developmental psychologist interested in the motor development of human infants observed 100 infants over the first year of life to determine the age in weeks at which a child could perform various motor behaviors such as crawling, walking with support, climbing stairs, walking alone, and so forth. Then the average age at which children could perform the various behaviors was computed and considered to be the *norm*.

Determine

    a.   the population of interest.

    b.   whether the population is finite or infinite.

    c.   whether the group on which the measures are taken constitute the population or a sample.

    d.   if the measurements made on the group refer to statistics or parameters.

    e. which of the three ways statistics is referred to (for example, numerical data).

    f. why statistics are being used (for example, evaluating research).

    g. whether reference is to descriptive or inferential statistics, or both.

    h. the numerical data.

    i. the sample size (if appropriate).

    j. the sample statistics mentioned (if appropriate).

MEETING THE CHALLENGE OF STATISTICS

The data sets described in this section will be used for problems in the **Meeting the Challenge of Statistics** section of *each chapter* of the Workbook.

New learning does not occur during sleep. Sleep, however, may be a very favorable state for processing newly acquired information. Insects, rats, and humans appear to show better retention of a newly learned event if they go to sleep immediately after the event than if they remain awake. One possible explanation for the better retention is that during sleep there is no opportunity for additional learning to interfere with the processing of the newly acquired information. A student interested in memory decides to conduct an experiment to see if sleeping immediately after a learning event will affect retention of the event for freshman students at the university. After receiving approval for the university's ethics review committee to conduct the research, the student obtains from the registrar a listing of all the freshmen enrolled at the university. The student assigns a number to each freshman, writes the individual numbers on slips of paper, and places the slips of paper in a box. The student vigorously shakes the box to thoroughly mix up the slips of paper and then selects, one at a time, sixty slips of paper from the box putting them into three piles of 20 each. Each pile represents a different group of freshman. The student researcher contacts the freshmen who agree to participate in the experiment.

The slips of paper representing each group of 20 freshman are put into a box and again withdrawn one at a time. These are placed in piles of 10 to represent two subgroups for each group of 20 freshmen. One of each of these two subgroups is designated the experimental group, the group that goes to sleep immediately after the learning event. The second of each of these two subgroups is designated the control group, the group that remains awake after the learning event. The student researcher decides on three different types of learning events, a different type to be presented to each of the original three groups of 20 freshmen, that is, to each set of experimental and control groups. The learning event for one set is a list of 20 nonsense syllables where each syllable consists of three consonants that have little or no meaning to the subjects. The learning event for the second set of experimental and control groups is a list of 20 emotionally neutral words such as "long." The learning event for the third set is a list of 20 emotion laden words, half of which are emotionally pleasant such as "happy" and half emotionally unpleasant such as "sad."

In the evening each freshman is presented the list until it is learned to one perfect recitation. The experimental groups then go to sleep whereas the control groups engage in some other activity such as reading or watching TV for at least one hour before going to sleep. The next morning each student is asked to recall as many of the syllables or words as possible. The following are the number of syllables or words correctly recalled by the freshmen in each set of experimental and control groups:

Nonsense Syllables
Experimental: 12, 13, 11, 11, 9, 10, 13, 12, 12, 10
Control: 10, 11, 9, 9, 6, 11, 6, 5, 8, 8

Emotionally Neutral Words
Experimental: 12, 14, 13, 10, 14, 15, 11, 13, 16, 15
Control: 10, 11, 12, 8, 9, 9, 9, 8, 11, 9

Emotion Laden Words (pleasant, **unpleasant)**
Experimental: (9,**6**), (10,8), (9,**7**), (8,**8**), (7,**6**), (9,**7**), (10,**6**), (8,**5**), (7,**8**), (9,**9)**
Control: (7,**5**), (9,**5**), (6,**5**), (7,**6**), (8,**7**), (7,**7**), (6,**7**), (9,**4**), (6,**5**), (5,**7**)

Chapter 1

For these data sets determine

1. the population of interest.

2. whether the population is finite or infinite.

3. whether the group(s) on which the measures are taken constitute a population or sample(s).

4. if measures made on the group(s) refer to statistics or parameters.

5. which of the three ways statistics is referred to (for example, measures of group characteristics).

6. why statistics are being used (for example, thinking and problem solving.

7. whether reference is to descriptive or inferential statistics.

8. the numerical data.

9. sample size.

10. the sample statistic(s) mentioned (if appropriate).

CHAPTER 2
DATA COLLECTION

DETAILED TEXTBOOK OUTLINE

Chapter 2

KEY TERMS AND DEFINITIONS

biased sample A sample that reflects only certain aspects of a
    population and is not representative of the entire
    population.

continuous variable A quantitative variable whose values fall
    at any point along an unbroken numerical scale of values.

correlational study A method of data collection in which two or
    more operationally defined dependent variables are measured
    to see if they are related in a systematic fashion.

dependent measures These are obtained measures of the
    characteristic(s) of interest in an experiment and a
    correlational study.

dependent or related samples Samples selected in such a way
    that assignment to one sample directly determines which
    member will be assigned to another sample.

dependent variable(s) The characteristic(s) of interest in an
    experiment or a correlational study.

discrete variable A quantitative variable whose values fall
    only at particular points along a numerical measurement
    scale.

independent samples Samples selected in such a way that
    assignment to one sample in no way affects how members are
    assigned to another sample.

independent variable The variable manipulated in an experiment
    that is assumed to potentially affect the dependent
    variable.

interval scale A scale of measurement that has an underlying
    quantitative dimension where the scale's basic units are
    equally dispersed throughout the dimension and where each
    unit represents an equal amount of the characteristic being
    measured.

levels The term used to indicate an investigator's manipulation
    of the independent variable(s) in an experiment.

nominal scale A system of numerical notation that places a
    characteristic of interest into a specific category.

operational definition A definition of a term based on imposed
    conditions or based on measurements used to identify the
    term in such a way that the definition of the term is clear
    and unambiguous.

ordinal scale A system of numerical notation in which a number represents the relative amount of a particular observable characteristic.

qualitative variable A variable having no consistent numerically identifiable characteristics that represent distinct events.

quantitative variable A variable that is defined on the basis of a measurable numerical value.

random sample A sample selected in such a way that every member of a given population has an equal chance of being selected and that every possible sample of the same size has an equal chance of being selected.

randomization The procedure by which members of a limited pool are randomly assigned without replacement to different samples.

randomized samples Samples formed when a limited pool is divided in such a way that each member of the pool has an equal chance of being assigned to any division and each set of members has an equal chance of forming any of the divisions.

ratio scale A scale of measurement containing an underlying quantitative dimension divided into equal quantitative units with an absolute zero point.

real limits The values one-half the unit of measurement above (upper real limit) and one-half the unit of measurement below (lower real limit) the estimated measured discrete value of the continuous variable.

research hypothesis A statement describing the relationship between the variables of interest in either an experiment or correlational study that can be tested empirically.

sampling with replacement A procedure used in selecting random samples whereby each member of the population selected for the sample is placed back into the population before the next member is selected.

sampling without replacement A procedure used in selecting random samples where once a member of the population is selected for the sample, it is removed from the population.

X Symbol used to represent the individual values of a set of dependent measures.

Y Symbol used to represent the individual values of a second set of dependent measures.

Chapter 2

MASTERING THE LANGUAGE OF STATISTICS

Fill-in-the-Blanks

Write the appropriate term(s) in the space(s) provided.

When a sample is selected from a population for the purpose of
making accurate and efficient judgments about the population, it
should not be a _____ sample. A _____ sample is a sample that
is not representative of the entire population. One type of
sample that is considered to be representative of the entire
population is called a _____ sample. A _____ _____ is a
subset of a population that has been selected in such a way that
every member of the population has an equal chance of being in
the subset. A random sample can be selected by sampling with or
without _____. Sampling _____ replacement is a
procedure that requires a population member to be placed back
into the population for further draws once it has been selected
as a sample member. Sampling _____ replacement requires that
a member not be returned to the population once it has been
selected as a sample member. Sampling _____ replacement is
usually not desired by most investigators. When two or more
random samples are formed from a limited pool of population
members, sampling _____ replacement is the procedure followed.
Random samples formed from a limited pool are called _____
samples. The procedure by which members of a limited pool are
randomly assigned without replacement to different samples is
called _____. Randomized samples can be _____,
that is, samples whose assignment of members has no effect on

the assignment of members to other samples, or _____, that
is, samples whose assignment of members influences the formation
of other samples.

Random and randomized samples are formed for the purpose of
describing events or characteristics of members of samples
(_____ statistics) or populations (_____ statistics).
Generally, these events or characteristics are described in a
clear and unambiguous way in terms of the conditions imposed to
produce them, or in terms of measurements used to quantify them.
Such clear and unambiguous definitions are called _____
definitions. The event or characteristic being described is
called the _____ variable. A _____ refers to any event
or characteristic that can take on more than one specific value.
Variables are classified as qualitative or _____. A
_____ variable is one that has no consistent numerically
identifiable characteristics. In contrast, a _____
variable is defined on the basis a numerical measurement.
Gender, marital status, and religious preference are examples of
_____ variables. Age, test score, and heartrate are
examples of _____ variables. Quantitative variables can
be either discrete or _____.

A _____ quantitative variable is one that can take on
any value within its limits. For example, weight as measured on
a balance is a _____ variable. A _____ quantitative
variable, on the other hand, can only take on certain values
within its limits. Family size, for example, is a _____
variable. The values that a variable can take on constitute a

scale of measurement. There are four scales of measurement:

_____, _____, _____, and _____. The numbers on a(n)

_____ scale simply name or label different levels of the

variable. The numbers on a(n) _____ scale represent the

relative amount of different levels of the variable. If each

basic unit along the scale represents an equal amount of the

characteristic being measured, the scale is either a(n)

_____ or _____ scale. If, in addition to the basic

units of the scale representing equal amounts of the

characteristic being measured, the zero point reflects the

absence of the measured characteristic, the scale is a _____

scale. If the zero point on the scale is arbitrary, the scale

could be _____, _____, or _____. A(n) _____

zero point allows proportional comparisons to be made between

levels of the variable. Measures of the characteristic of

interest or _____ variable are called _____ measures.

The symbol used to represent the value of the _____ measure

is the letter ____. In an experiment these measures are assumed

to be influenced by the _____ variable. The _____

variable is something that the experimenter manipulates. Giving

different doses of a drug to different groups of subjects to

assess the effect on blood pressure is an example of

manipulating a(n) _____ variable. The different doses

of the drug constitute the different _____ of the _____

variable. Blood pressure is the _____ variable and the

numbers used to express blood pressure are the _____

measures. A statement of the relationship between drug dosage and blood pressure level in a way that it can be empirically tested is called a research _____. In an experiment the _____ hypothesis is a statement about the relationship of the _____ variable to the _____ variable. In contrast, in a correlational study, the _____ hypothesis is a statement of the relationship between two _____ variables or _____. A _____ _____ is a method of data collection in which two or more operationally defined dependent variables are measured to see if they are related in a systematic fashion. In a correlational study, a measurement taken on one dependent variable is symbolized by _____ and a measurement taken on the other is symbolized by _____. If the measures of the dependent variables are continuous then they will have _____ _____, which are the values that are one-half the unit of measurement above and one-half the unit of measurement below the estimated measured discrete value of the variable. The values one-half the unit above the measured discrete values are _____ _____ _____. The values one-half the unit below the measured discrete values are _____ _____ _____.

True-False Items

Place a T for true or an F for false in the space provided before each item.

1. ____ A sample that reflects only certain aspects of a population and is not representative of the entire population is a random sample.

2. ____ A system of numerical notation in which a number represents the relative amount of a particular characteristic is called a nominal scale.

3.____ A quantitative variable whose points fall only at particular points along a numerical measurement scale is a discrete variable.

4.____ Samples selected in such a way that assignment to one sample directly determines which member will be assigned to another sample are related samples.

5.____ Another name for related samples is dependent samples.

6.____ Randomization is the procedure by which members of a limited pool are assigned with replacement to different samples.

7.____ A method of data collection in which two or more operationally defined dependent variables are measured to see if they are related in a systematic fashion is called an experiment.

8.____ The real limits of a number are the values obtained for the dependent measures.

9.____ An ordinal scale has an absolute zero point.

10.____ Both interval and ratio scales have an arbitrary zero point.

11.____ Operational definitions are clear but ambiguous.

12.____ Independent variables are measurements made on independent samples.

Multiple-Choice Items

Blacken out the letter corresponding to the correct answer.

1. The scale of measurement not represented in the statement *The race car driver in car number 37 came in second and won $5000.00* is
   (a) nominal.
   (b) ordinal.
   (c) interval.
   (d) ratio.

2. A quantitative variable whose values fall at any point along an unbroken numerical scale of values is a(n) _____ variable.
   (a) dependent
   (b) independent
   (c) discrete
   (d) continuous

3. Samples selected in such a way that assignment to one sample in no way affects how members are assigned to another sample are
    (a) random.
    (b) biased.
    (c) randomized.
    (d) independent.

4. A scale of measurement that has an underlying quantitative dimension where the scale's basic units are equally dispersed throughout the dimension and where each unit represents an equal amount of the characteristic being measured is a(n)
    (a) nominal scale.
    (b) interval scale.
    (c) ratio scale.
    (d) both b and c.

5. The term used to indicate an investigator's manipulation of the independent variable in an experiment is
    (a) experimentation.
    (b) randomization.
    (c) sampling with replacement.
    (d) levels.

6. A variable having no consistent numerically identifiable characteristics that represent distinct events is a(n)
    (a) continuous variable.
    (b) independent variable.
    (c) qualitative variable.
    (d) Y-variable.

7. The characteristic of interest in an experiment is called the
    (a) independent variable.
    (b) levels.
    (c) research hypothesis.
    (d) dependent variable.

8. The amount of change in the pockets of each student in your statistics class cannot
    (a) be measured along a ratio scale.
    (b) be a discrete variable.
    (c) have real limits.
    (d) be a dependent measure.

9. Samples formed when a limited pool is divided in such a way that each member of the pool has an equal chance of being assigned to any division and each set of members has an equal chance of forming any of the divisions are
    (a) random samples.
    (b) randomized samples.
    (c) biased samples.

   (d) dependent samples.

10. A procedure used in selecting samples whereby once a member
    of the population is selected for a sample it is removed
    from the population is called
    (a) random sampling.
    (b) randomization.
    (c) sampling with replacement.
    (d) sampling without replacement.

11. Assigning the number one to sparrows, the number two to
    bluejays, the number three to robins, and the number four to
    blackbirds is an example of
    (a) a nominal scale.
    (b) an ordinal scale.
    (c) an interval scale.
    (d) a ratio scale.

12. Anything that can take on more than one specific value is
    called
    (a) a dependent measure.
    (b) real limits.
    (c) levels.
    (d) a variable.

APPLYING STATISTICAL CONCEPTS

Example Application

Obsessions are recurrent thoughts or impulses that a person has
difficulty controlling. Compulsions are repetitive behaviors
that are generally consequences of the obsessions. For example,
an individual obsessed with the thought of having left the front
door unlocked at night may be compelled to repeatedly check the
door before retiring for the night. A psychiatrist who believes
that behavior therapy is different from psychotherapy in
alleviating the obsessive-compulsive disorder randomly divides
sixty clients suffering from the disorder into two equal size
groups. The psychiatrist uses the behavior therapy to treat the
subjects in one group and psychotherapy to treat the subjects in
the other group. The number of therapy sessions required to
alleviate each client's suffering, which is when the client
maintains therapy is no longer necessary because the obsessive
thoughts and compulsive behaviors no longer occur, is recorded.
To summarize the data for each group the psychiatrist averages
the number of sessions required to alleviate the disorder.
     If you can apply what you have learned so far to this
situation you know that the psychiatrist is conducting an
experiment because the effect of the manipulation of an
independent variable (type of therapy) on a **dependent variable**
(client's suffering) is being assessed. The independent

variable is a **qualitative** variable with just two **levels**,
behavior therapy and psychotherapy. The **operational definition**
of the dependent variable is in terms of the **dependent measure**,
the number of sessions required for the client to report the
obsessive-compulsive behavior no longer occurs (symbolized by
X). The dependent variable is a **discrete** variable measured
along a **ratio** scale. Because the dependent variable is a
discrete variable, there are no **real limits** of the dependent
measures. The psychiatrist's clients represent a **biased sample**
because the clients of only one psychiatrist probably reflect
only certain aspects of the **population** of people suffering from
an obsessive-compulsive disorder. The psychiatrist, however,
used **randomized samples** (*N* = 30 each), so the **statistics**
(averages) computed for the experiment can be used to make
judgments about measures (**parameters**) of the **finite population**
represented by the clients in the experiment (**inferential
statistics**), or simply to describe and summarize the data for
the two **samples** of clients (**descriptive statistics**). The
information collected in this experiment (**numerical data**) is
used to compute measures (**statistics**) of the characteristic of
interest (average number of sessions) so that the psychiatrist
can make judgements about the population represented by these
specific clients and reach a conclusion about his **research
hypothesis**: behavior therapy differs from psychotherapy in
alleviating an obsessive-compulsive disorder. Thus the term
"**statistics**" is used in all of the following ways (1) as
numerical data; (2) as a measure of group characteristics; and
(3) as a branch of mathematics that deals with describing,
summarizing, analyzing, and interpreting numerical data.

Application Exercises

1. An educational psychologist believes that there is a
   relationship between the intelligence of children and their
   parents. To test this belief, five thousand high school
   seniors are randomly selected from high schools throughout
   the United States and are given an I.Q test. One of their
   parents is randomly selected to participate in the study and
   is also given an I.Q test. The number of points scored on
   this test is considered an indicator of intelligence.

   Determine whether reference is made to

   a. descriptive or inferential statistics, or both.

   b. samples, populations, or both—if sample(s), specify
      whether they are biased, random, or randomized, and
      dependent or independent; if populations, specify
      whether they are finite or infinite.

    c.   parameters, statistics, or both—for statistics, specify whether they are numerical data or measures of group characteristics.

    d.   experiment or correlational study.

    e.   independent variable(s)—if so, specify levels.

    f.   dependent variable(s).

    g.   dependent measure—if so, specify whether it is qualitative or quantitative, and discrete or continuous; also specify the scale of measurement.

    h.   real limits.

    i.   operational definition(s)—if so, describe them.

    j.   a research hypothesis—if so, describe it.

2. Learning a list of items (for example, nonsense syllables) in the order in which they are presented is referred to as serial-order learning. The most well known and important finding from research on serial-order learning is that items in the middle of the list are learned more slowly than items at the ends of the list. This is called the serial-position effect. A learning psychologist believes that the serial-position effect can be altered by strategically placing an attention-getting stimulus (for example a bold face syllable) near the center of the list. To test this belief the psychologist randomly selects two groups of fifteen students from the school's roster. One group is presented a list of words without the attention-getting stimulus in the middle of the list. The second group is presented the same list with a bold face item (attention-getting

stimulus) near the center of the list. Each subject is presented the list one time and asked to recall the list in the order in which the items were presented. The average number of errors at each serial-position of the item is computed for each group and compared.

Determine whether reference is made to

a. descriptive or inferential statistics, or both.

b. samples, populations, or both—if sample(s), specify whether they are biased, random, or randomized, and dependent or independent; if populations, specify whether they are finite or infinite.

c. parameters, statistics, or both—for statistics, specify whether they are numerical data or measures of group characteristics.

d. experiment or correlational study.

e. independent variable(s)—if so, specify levels.

f. dependent variable(s).

g. dependent measure—if so, specify whether it is qualitative or quantitative, and discrete or continuous; also specify the scale of measurement.

h. real limits.

i. operational definition(s)—if so, describe them.

   j. a research hypothesis—if so, describe it.

MEETING THE CHALLENGE OF STATISTICS

The following problems pertain to the memory experiment
described in the *Meeting the Challenge of Statistics* section in
Chapter 1 of this workbook. Examine the data set described on
pages 9-10 of this workbook in order to answer the following.

1. Define the population of interest.

2. State whether the population is finite or infinite.

3. State whether the overall sample of sixty freshmen selected
   from the population is biased or random.

4. State whether selection of this sample is sampling with or
   without replacement.

5. Describe two other ways a random sample of sixty freshmen
   could have been selected from the specified population.

6. State whether the three samples selected from the pool of
   sixty freshmen are biased, random, or randomized. Explain
   your answer.

7. State the size of the three samples.

8. Are the three samples dependent or independent samples?

9. Give a reason for your answer to problem 8.

10. Form a research hypothesis.

11. Operationally define the independent variable.

12. Operationally define the dependent variable.

13. Operationally define "emotionally pleasant."

14. Specify the dependent measure.

15. State whether the dependent measure is qualitative or quantitative. Explain your answer.

16. If the dependent measure is quantitative, specify the scale of measurement.

17. State whether the dependent measure is continuous or discrete. Explain your answer.

18. State whether or not the dependent measure has real limits. Give the reason for your answer.

19. On which sample are two dependent measures taken?

20. Specify the two dependent measures referred to in problem 19.

CHAPTER 3
ORGANIZING A SET OF DATA: TABLE FORMAT

DETAILED TEXTBOOK OUTLINE

Chapter 3

KEY TERMS AND DEFINITIONS

array An arrangement of data organized from the highest numerical value to the lowest.

class intervals Groups that are numerically defined in such a way that any given raw score can belong to one and only one of the groups.

class interval width The distance between the lower real limit of the class and the upper real limit of the class.

cumulative frequency distribution A frequency distribution that includes a running total of frequencies at each score or interval starting at the lowest score or class interval.

frequency The number of times a particular raw score occurs, symbolized by f.

grouped frequency distribution An arrangement of data organized on the basis of mutually exclusive groups of raw scores called class intervals. The number of times each raw score occurs within a class interval is determined and listed as the frequency of the interval.

i Symbol for the interval width.

$i = URL - LRL$ Formula for obtaining i.

k A symbol used to refer to the number of class intervals in a grouped frequency distribution.

lower apparent limit The lowest score value associated with a particular class interval.

midpoint of a class interval The middle score value of a class interval obtained by summing either real or apparent limits and dividing by 2.

percent cumulative frequency distribution A frequency distribution in which cumulative frequency is expressed as a percentage.

range/$i \approx k$ Formula used to approximate a value of k when forming a grouped frequency distribution.

range of raw scores A value indicating the amount of

dispersion among the raw scores. It is obtained by subtracting the lower real limit of the lowest raw score from the upper real limit of the highest score.

raw data or raw scores Data as originally collected.

relative frequency distribution A frequency distribution in which frequency is expressed as a percent of the total frequency.

simple frequency distribution An arrangement of data organized on the basis of the number of times each raw score occurs.

$\sum$ A summation symbol.

upper and lower real limits of a class interval One half of the unit of measurement above and below the upper and lower apparent limits, respectively.

URL and *LRL* Symbols for the upper real limit and lower real limit of a class interval, respectively.

upper apparent limit The highest score value associated with a particular class interval.

X' Symbol for the midpoint of a class interval.

MASTERING THE LANGUAGE OF STATISTICS

Fill-in-the-blanks

Write the appropriate term(s) in the space(s) provided.

Data as originally collected are referred to as _____ data.

Since it is difficult to extract information readily from

raw data, the _____ scores are often organized in a table

format. The simplest way to organize the raw scores in a

table format is to form a(n) _____. In forming a(n)

_____ the raw scores are arranged from the highest

numerical value to the lowest. The distance between the

lower real limit of the lowest numerical value and the upper
real limit of the highest numerical value is called the
_____ of the raw scores. The _____ of the raw scores
indicates the amount of dispersion among the raw scores.
Although a(n) _____ allows you to determine readily the
highest and lowest score and quickly calculate the _____
of the raw scores, it does not provide a very accurate
impression of how the scores are distributed throughout the
scale of measurement. A more accurate impression of how the
scores are distributed can be obtained by arranging the data
into a _____ _____ distribution. A _____
_____ distribution organizes data in table format on
the basis of the number of times each raw score occurs. The
raw scores in a simple frequency distribution are symbolized
by _____. The number of times each score occurs is
referred to as its _____. A raw score's frequency
is symbolized by the English letter ____. In a simple
frequency distribution, then, every possible _____ _____
between the highest and lowest obtained raw scores is listed
in the column labeled X and the _____ of each possible
score is listed in the column labeled f. The sum of the
frequencies, symbolized _____, should equal the sample
size, N.

When there is a large number of raw scores, organizing
the data as a _____ _____ distribution does not

adequately reveal group patterns. Instead, scores are
generally assigned to mutually exclusive classes called
_____ _____. These _____ _____ are
groups that are numerically defined in such a way that any
given raw score can belong to one and only one of the
groups. An organization of data into class intervals with
the number of raw scores within a class listed as its
frequency is called a _____ frequency distribution.
The number of class intervals in a grouped frequency
distribution is symbolized by k. The highest and lowest
scores represented in the class interval are the _____ and
_____ apparent limits, respectively. One half the unit
of measurement above and below the upper and lower apparent
limits, respectively, are the _____ limits of the interval.
The _____ real limit is a half-unit of measurement above
the _____ apparent limit and the _____ real limit is a
half-unit of measurement below the _____ apparent limit.
The upper and lower real limits are symbolized _____ and
_____, respectively.

Each class interval also has a midpoint and a width
symbolized by _____ and _____, respectively. The
_____ of a class interval is the middle score value and is
obtained by summing either the _____ or _____
limits and dividing by two. The _____ of a class
interval, symbolized by i, is calculated by subtracting the

_____ real limit from the _____ real limit. The width
is used in conjunction with the range to obtain an
approximate value of _____. The formula for approximating
k is _____.

   Other types of _____ distributions that can be
constructed are relative, cumulative, and percent cumulative
frequency distributions. A frequency distribution that
includes a column in which each frequency is expressed as a
percent of the total frequency is called a _____
frequency distribution. One that contains a column in which
there is a running total of frequencies at each class
interval or score beginning at the lowest interval or score
is called a _____ frequency distribution. If the
running totals of frequencies are converted to values
indicating the percentage of scores falling at or below the
corresponding score or class interval, then the distribution
is called a _____ _____ frequency distribution.

True-False Items

*Place a T for true or an F for false in the space provided
before each item.*

1. _____ An array arranges all possible numbers between the
highest and lowest obtained number.

2. _____ The width of a class interval can be obtained by
subtracting the lower apparent limit from the upper
apparent limit.

3. _____ The symbol k represents the class interval width.

4. ____ The midpoint of a class interval can be obtained by adding the upper and lower real limits and dividing by two.

5. ____ *URL* – *LRL* is the formula for obtaining i.

6. ____ A frequency distribution in which cumulative frequency is expressed as a percentage is a cumulative frequency distribution.

7. ____ The upper apparent limit is one half-unit of measurement above the upper real limit.

8. ____ Groups that are numerically defined in such a way that any given raw score can belong to one and only one group are called class intervals.

9. ____ The number of times a particular score occurs is symbolized f.

10. ____ Frequency expressed as a percent of the total frequency is called relative frequency.

11. ____ The symbol for the midpoint of a class interval is X'.

12. ____ Range/$i \approx k$.

Multiple-Choice Items

Blacken out the letter corresponding to the correct answer.

1. A frequency distribution in which frequency is expressed as a percent of the total frequency is a _____ frequency distribution.
   (a) simple
   (b) grouped
   (c) relative
   (d) cumulative

2. The symbol for the number of class intervals is
   (a) k.
   (b) i.
   (c) X'.
   (d) f.

3. *URL* – *LRL* is
   (a) the width of class interval.
   (b) the distance between the lower and upper real limits of a class interval.

(c) the formula for determining the value of i.
(d) all of the above.

4. The lowest score value associated with a particular class interval is called
   (a) a lower real limit.
   (b) a lower apparent limit.
   (c) the zero point.
   (d) none of the above.

5. A value indicating the amount of dispersion among scores is
   (a) Σf.
   (b) the range.
   (c) k.
   (d) URL.

6. An arrangement of data organized from the highest numerical value to the lowest is called
   (a) a simple frequency distribution.
   (b) a grouped frequency distribution.
   (c) an array.
   (d) raw data.

7. The summation symbol is
   (a) Σ.
   (b) μ.
   (c) X'.
   (d) k.

8. The midpoint of a class interval is
   (a) $(URL + LRL)/2$.
   (b) X'.
   (c) the sum of the upper and lower apparent limits divided by two.
   (d) all of the above.

9. An arrangement of data organized on the basis of the number of times each score occurs is
   (a) an array.
   (b) a simple frequency distribution.
   (c) raw data.
   (d) none of the above.

10. A frequency distribution that includes a running total of frequencies at each interval, starting at the lowest class interval is a
    (a) cumulative frequency distribution.
    (b) grouped frequency distribution.
    (c) percent cumulative frequency distribution.

(d) relative frequency distribution.

11. The symbol for the number of times a particular raw score occurs is
    (a) f.
    (b) k.
    (c) i.
    (d) Σ.

12. A frequency distribution in which cumulative frequency is expressed as a percentage is
    (a) a relative frequency distribution.
    (b) a cumulative frequency distribution.
    (c) a grouped frequency distribution.
    (d) none of the above

APPLYING STATISTICAL CONCEPTS

Example Application

A developmental psychologist interested in the time children between the ages of 5 and 7 spend watching television asked the mothers of sixty children in grades kindergarten through second how many hours on the average their children spend watching TV each week. These data were organized as the grouped frequency distribution in Table 3.1 with additional columns indicating relative frequency (**rel** f), cumulative frequency (**cum** f), and percent cumulative frequency (**% cum** f).

Table 3.1
Grouped Frequency Distribution of the Number of Hours on the Average a Sample of Five to Seven-Year-Old Children Watch Television Each Week ($N = 60$)

Class Interval	f	rel f	cum f	% cum
33 - 35	1	1.7	60	100.0
30 - 32	2	3.3	59	98.3
27 - 29	1	1.7	57	95.0
24 - 26	5	8.3	56	93.3
21 - 23	8	13.3	51	85.0
18 - 20	8	13.3	43	71.7
15 - 17	16	26.7	35	58.3
12 - 14	10	16.7	19	31.7
09 - 11	5	8.3	9	15.0
06 - 08	3	5.0	4	6.7
03 - 05	1	1.7	1	1.7

Having covered the chapter on organizing data in table format you should know that the sample size of the five to seven-year-old children is too large to organize the data as an **array** or as a **simple frequency distribution**. You should recognize that the organization of the data in Table 3.1 follows the conventions for presenting data in table format. The table has the word "Table" followed by a specific identification number (Table 3.1), and there is a brief description of the information provided in the table. The data presented in the table are clearly labeled with column headings. Also, the abbreviations used as column headings are identified in the table heading.

You should also recognize that the organization of data in Table 3.1 follows the conventions for constructing a **grouped frequency distribution** in the absence of designated external criteria. The grouped frequency distribution has k, the number of class intervals, within the prescribed limits ($10 \le k \le 20$), and both the highest and lowest classes have $f > 0$. The interval width ($i = 3$) is one of the preferred values (1, 2, 3, 4, 5, or multiples of 5), and the **lower apparent limits** are multiples of i. You should know that the distance between the midpoints (X') of the class intervals also equals i and that the i for any given class equals **URL - LRL**. You should check to see that the sum of the **frequency** column (Σf) equals the sample size, N. You should also check to see that the sum of the **relative frequency** column equals 100 and that the *rel f* for each class is obtained by dividing the frequency of the class by Σf and multiplying the quotient by 100. Likewise, the **percent cumulative frequency** of a class equals (*cum f*)/Σf multiplied by 100. You should recall that **cumulative frequency** is a running total of frequencies at each class interval beginning with the lowest class.

Application Exercises

1. Assume that an instructor of a large principles of psychology class wants an indication of the type of student enrolled in the class in terms of intelligence. Sixteen students volunteer to take an IQ test given by the instructor. The scores on the test were 130, 128, 120, 120, 119, 119, 119, 115, 110, 110, 110, 100, 100, 100, 100, 100. The instructor averages the scores to get an indication of the average intelligence of the class.

Determine

a. the population of interest.

b. the type (descriptive, inferential, or both) of statistics being used.

c. the type (biased, random, randomized) of sample(s), if any, referred to.

d. the type (experimental, correlational) of design, if any.

e. independent variables, if any.

f. scale of measurement.

g. an operational definition of the dependent variable or measure.

h. type of organization, if any, for example, raw data, array, or frequency distribution (if frequency distribution specify type, simple, grouped, cumulative, relative, or percent cumulative).

i. f for the lowest class or score.

j. the size of i, if appropriate.

k. upper apparent limit of the highest class or score.

l. $rel\ f$ for the second highest class or score.

m. LRL and URL for the lowest class or score.

    n. the range of the scores.

    o. X' of the highest class, if appropriate.

    p. k, if any.

    q. % *cum f* for the third highest class or score.

    r. *cum f* for the second lowest class or score.

2. An investigator of animal behavior wants to determine how much water rats will drink in the first hour after delivery from a commercial supplier of laboratory rodents. Ninety rats are ordered and upon delivery are placed individually in a standard suspended rodent cage for one hour with food and water freely available. The amount of water consumed by each rat is determined from the measured amounts of water at the beginning and end of the hour period. The collected data are organized in Table 3.2.

Table 3.2
The Amount of Water Consumed by 90 Rats During the First Hour after Delivery from a Commercial Supplier

Class Interval	Frequency (f)
27 – 29	3
24 – 26	5
21 – 23	11
18 – 20	10
15 – 17	10
12 – 14	17
09 – 11	13
06 – 08	11
03 – 05	8
00 – 02	2

Determine

    a. the population of interest.

b. the type (descriptive, inferential, or both) of statistics being used.

c. the type (biased, random, randomized) of sample(s), if any, referred to.

d. the type (experimental, correlational) of design, if any.

e. independent variables, if any.

f. scale of measurement.

g. an operational definition of the dependent variable or measure.

h. type of organization, if any, for example, raw data, array, or frequency distribution (if frequency distribution, specify type, simple, grouped, cumulative, relative, or percent cumulative).

i. f for the lowest class or score.

j. the size of i, if appropriate.

k. upper apparent limit of the highest class or score.

l. $rel\ f$ for the second highest class or score.

m. LRL and URL for the lowest class or score.

   n.   the range of the scores.

   o.   *X'* of the highest class, if appropriate.

   p.   *k*, if any.

   q.   % *cum f* for the third highest class or score.

   r.   *cum f* for the second lowest class or score.

MEETING THE CHALLENGE OF STATISTICS

The following problems pertain to the memory experiment described in the *Meeting the Challenge of Statistics* section in Chapter 1, pages 9-10, of this workbook. The number of syllables or words correctly recalled by the freshmen in each set of experimental and control groups reproduced from Chapter 1 are as follows:

Nonsense Syllables
Experimental: 12, 13, 11, 11, 9, 10, 13, 12, 12, 10
Control: 10, 11, 9, 9, 6, 11, 6, 5, 8, 8

Emotionally Neutral Words
Experimental: 12, 14, 13, 10, 14, 15, 11, 13, 16, 15
Control: 10, 11, 12, 8, 9, 9, 9, 8, 11, 9

Emotion Laden Words (pleasant, **unpleasant)**
Experimental: (9,**6**), (10,**8**), (9,**7**), (8,8), (7,**6**), (9,**7**), (10,**6**), (8,**5**), (7,**8**), (9,**9)**
Control: (7,**5**), (9,**5**), (6,**5**), (7,6), (8,**7**), (7,**7**), (6,**7**), (9,**4**), (6,**5**), (5,**7**)

   1. State the type of organization presented, if any, of the data from the experimental group presented with the nonsense syllables.

   2. Organize into an array the 20 scores from the group presented with the emotionally neutral words.

3. Add the scores for each subject presented with the emotion laden words and then organize the 60 scores from the entire sample of freshmen into a simple frequency distribution.

4. Add to the simple frequency distribution of problem 3 a relative frequency column.

5. Determine the range of the raw scores.

6. Organize the data from the entire sample of freshman into a grouped frequency distribution with the designated criteria of $i = 2$ and $k = 8$.

7. Add to the grouped frequency distribution of problem 6 a cumulative frequency column.

8. Organize the data from the entire sample of freshmen into a grouped frequency distribution with the designated criteria of $i = 2$ and $k = 7$.

9. Convert the grouped frequency distribution of problem 8 to a percent cumulative frequency distribution.

10. Give the *LRL* and *URL* of the highest class interval in the frequency distribution of problem 6.

11. Compute *X′* for the highest class interval for the frequency distribution of problem 8.

CHAPTER 4
ORGANIZING A SET OF DATA: GRAPHS AND DISPLAYS

DETAILED TEXTBOOK OUTLINE

Chapter 4

KEY TERMS AND DEFINITIONS

bar graph A graph used to display discrete variables where height of each discrete bar represents the frequency or a measure of each observed characteristic.

display A pictorial organization of raw scores that reveals group patterns or trends.

figure A graph format of data organization that includes a label number and caption describing information presented.

frequency polygon A graph used to display continuous variables where adjoining points, which represent the frequency of each observed characteristic, are connected by straight lines that are anchored to the X-axis.

graph A diagrammatic representation of group patterns or trends.

histogram A graph used to display continuous variables where the height of each adjoining bar represents the frequency of each observed characteristic and the height and area of which are proportional to total frequency.

leaves The division of trailing digits of raw scores used to create stem-and-leaf displays.

line graph A graph used to display continuous variables where adjoining points, which represent summaries of measured values of specific characteristics, are connected by straight lines. It is used to depict trends in a dependent variable graphed as a function of an independent variable.

negatively skewed distribution An asymmetrical distribution where the greatest frequency of scores occurs for high scores and there is a trailing of frequencies at the low score values. Its frequency polygon would reveal a tail extended to the left of the graph toward the zero value of the X-axis.

percent cumulative frequency curve A graph used to display continuous variables where adjoining points connected by straight lines are used to represent the cumulative frequency (represented as a percent of the total frequency) of the observed characteristics.

positively skewed distribution An asymmetrical distribution where the greatest frequency of scores occurs for low scores and there is a trailing of frequencies at the high-score values. Its frequency polygon would reveal a tail extended to the right of the graph away from the zero value of the X-axis.

Chapter 4

scatter plot A graph showing the points representing each of the *X*- and *Y*-values obtained for dependent measures of a correlational study.

stem-and-leaf display A pictorial representation of group patterns using raw scores that includes a label number and a display heading describing the information presented.

stems The division of leading digits of raw scores used to form stem-and-leaf displays.

symmetrical distribution A distribution that has left- and right-half mirror images.

tails of a distribution Those areas of a frequency polygon at the left and right extremes of the distribution.

X-axis The horizontal axis of a graph.

Y-axis The vertical axis of a graph.

MASTERING THE LANGUAGE OF STATISTICS

Fill-in-the-Blanks

Write the appropriate term(s) in the space(s) provided.

In this chapter we focus on two procedures used to depict data, a diagram or _____ and a pictorial organization of raw data or a _____. It is always the case that a graph is presented as a _____. A _____ is a graph which includes a label number and caption which describes the information presented in the graph. A convention followed when constructing a figure is that the intersection of the __-___ (horizontal line) and the ___-____ (vertical line) reflects the zero point on both axes. Another convention is that the length of the *Y*-axis should be between 60 and 80 percent the total length of the ___-_____.

Frequency data can be depicted graphically in a variety of

forms. A _____ _____, for example, is a graph used to display values of discrete variables where the height of each bar represents the _____ of the observed characteristic. Another type of graph used to depict frequency data is the _____, a series of adjoining bars of equal width where the height of each bar represents the frequency and the area of the bar corresponds to relative frequency. In contrast to a _____ _____ which displays values of discrete variables, the _____ is used to depict group patterns for frequency data observed for a continuous variable. An alternative to the histogram is a _____ _____. A _____ _____, like the histogram, is a graph used to depict group patterns. The points in a _____ _____ are connected by straight lines and represent the frequencies of the scores or class intervals of a continuous variable. A _____ _____ _____ _____ is a graphic representation of a percent cumulative frequency distribution. The points in a _____ _____ _____ _____ represent percent cumulative frequencies of the scores or class intervals. The _____ _____ _____ _____ is used to present the relative standing of any particular score obtained when the variable of interest is a continuous variable.

　　There are many times when graphs are used to display data other than frequency counts. The _____ of a _____ _____, for example, can also be used to represent some measured characteristic (such as average salary) of a discrete variable (such as type of job). If the variable of interest is a continuous variable, then a _____ _____ is used to display some measured characteristic. A _____ _____ is used to depict trends in a dependent variable as a function of a(n)_____ variable. If, on the other hand, data are collected and organized for the purpose of depicting a relationship between two dependent variables, then a graph of the pairs of *X*- and *Y*-values is called a _____ _____. In a _____ _____ the *X*-axis and *Y*-axis are of equal length.

Because of the frequent occurrence of certain shapes of distributions, the graphs depicting the distributions as well as the distributions have been given certain descriptive labels. A _____ distribution, for example, is a distribution whose figure or graph is symmetrical, that is, whose right half is a mirror image of its left half. A _____ _____ distribution is a distribution in which the frequency of scores towards the right tail of the distribution is greater than the frequency towards the left tail of the distribution. In contrast a _____ _____ distribution is one in which there is greater concentration of scores towards the lower end or left tail of the distribution. The _____ of a distribution refer to those areas at the right and left extremes of the distribution.

A pictorial organization of scores that reveals group patterns is called a _____. A _____-and-_____ display is a pictorial representation of a distribution of scores that uses the individual raw scores to depict the group pattern. Each raw score is divided into leading digits called _____ and

trailing digits called _____. As with tables and figures,
a description of the _____ is required. The word
"_____", along with a number, a heading, and a units
scale appear at the top. The _____-and-_____ _____ is an
interesting method of presenting data because it allows an
investigator to maintain the identity of each data point while
revealing group patterns.

True-False Items

*Place a T for true or an F for false in the space provided
before each item.*

1.____ A bar graph is used to display continuous variables
where the height of each bar represents the frequency or
measure of each observed characteristic.

2.____ The divisions of leading digits of raw scores used to
form stem-and-leaf displays are called leaves.

3.____ A graph showing the points representing each of the *X*-
and *Y*-values obtained for dependent measures of a
correlational study is called a scatter plot.

4.____ The horizontal axis of a graph is the *X*-axis.

5.____ In a positively skewed distribution the concentration of
scores is towards the left tail of the distribution.

6.____ The areas of a frequency polygon at the left and right
extremes of the distribution are referred to as stems.

7.____ The graph used to depict a trend in a dependent variable
as a function of a continuous independent variable is
called a line graph.

8.____ The sides of the bars of a bar graph are not coincident
whereas those of a histogram are.

9.____ A distribution that has left- and right-half mirror
images is called a symmetrical distribution.

10.____ A frequency polygon that reveals a tail extended to the
right of the graph away from the intersection of the
axes would represent a positively skewed distribution.

11.____ The *Y*-axis of a graph is the vertical axis.

Chapter 4

12.____ A diagrammatic representation of group patterns or
        trends is called a figure.

Multiple-Choice Items

Blacken out the letter corresponding to the correct answer.

1. A format of data organization that includes a label number
   and description describing the information presented is
   (a) a table.
   (b) a figure.
   (c) a display.
   (d) all of the above.

2. Which of the following are not conventions to be followed in
   presenting data in graph format?
   (a) Describe each graph fully in a figure caption.
   (b) Proportion axes correctly.
   (c) For each set of scores indicate a clearly identified
       zero point.
   (d) Include a units scale at the top enabling anyone viewing
       the graph to determine the type of data collected.

3. In selecting the type of graph to construct it is *not*
   essential to consider
   (a) the purpose of organizing the data graphically.
   (b) the sample size.
   (c) whether the characteristic of interest is continuous or
       discrete.
   (d) whether the data collected are frequency data or
       quantitative measures such as IQ scores.

4. Which type of graph would be most appropriate for graphing
   the number of gallons of water used per week by a community
   over a ten-week period?
   (a) bar graph
   (b) histogram
   (c) scatter plot
   (d) line graph

5. The most probable shape of a distribution of scores on an
   easy statistics exam is
   (a) symmetrical.
   (b) negatively skewed.
   (c) positively skewed.
   (d) none of the above.

6. Given that an instructor is interested in displaying group
   patterns and the groups are based on letter grades, the most
   appropriate type of graph would be a
   (a) bar graph.
   (b) line graph.

(c) histogram.
(d) frequency polygon.

7. The stem is 12, the leaves are 24, and the unit of measurement is 0.01, therefore, the value represented by 12 4 would be
(a) 0.124.
(b) 1.24.
(c) 12.4.
(d) 124.

8. The most appropriate graph to depict an individual's relative standing among a group of individuals would be a
(a) bar graph.
(b) line graph.
(c) percent cumulative frequency curve.
(d) frequency polygon.

9. A graph depicting the relationship between height and weight for a sample of college students is a
(a) line graph.
(b) scatter plot.
(c) cumulative frequency curve.
(d) histogram.

10. The frequency of scores on a psychology exam by a large group of students would best be represented by a
(a) scatter plot.
(b) frequency polygon.
(c) line graph.
(d) percent cumulative frequency curve.

11. A distribution where the greatest frequency of scores occurs for high scores and there is a trailing off of frequencies at the low score values is
(a) positively skewed.
(b) negatively skewed.
(c) symmetrical.
(d) all of the above.

12. The label "Figure" and the figure number appear at
(a) the top of the figure above the figure caption.
(b) the top of the figure on the first line of the figure caption.
(c) the bottom of the figure and above the figure caption.
(d) the bottom of the figure on the first line of the figure caption.

APPLYING STATISTICAL CONCEPTS

Example Application

Chapter 4

Experience usually serves human beings well in problem solving. There are, however, times when our past experience can have negative consequences. One such negative consequence on problem solving is called functional fixedness. Functional fixedness refers to the thought or belief that an object has only its customary use. A person who needs a paper weight and fails to see that the empty water glass on the desk can serve that purpose demonstrates functional fixedness. A cognitive psychologist interested in factors that may overcome the effect of functional fixedness on problem solving uses a random numbers table to select 200 students from the school roster. The students are then randomly divided into two groups. One group is given 10 functional fixedness problems with no preliminary instructions other than to solve the problems. The second group is given the same ten problems with the preliminary instructions to pay attention to the materials on hand in solving the problem. Each student is given two minutes to solve each problem. The number of problems solved by each student is tabulated. The performances of the two groups are compared.

A number of things that you have learned in this and preceding chapters can be applied to this hypothetical situation. You should know that the method of data collection is **experimental**. You should also recognize that a **random sample** of students (**N** = 200) was **randomized** into two groups (**N** = 100 each) to be used in an experiment in which the **independent variable** was type of instructions and the **dependent measure** was the number of problems solved. The **dependent variable**, the degree of functional fixedness, can be **operationally defined** in terms of the measure used to quantify it (number of problems solved with fewer solved problems indicating a greater degree of functional fixedness). You should also recognize that the **dependent variable** is a **discrete variable** measured along a **ratio scale**. The type of graph that you would use to depict and compare the data from the two groups would be a **bar graph** because the **independent variable** (type of instructions) which is depicted along the **X-axis** is a **discrete qualitative variable**. The average number of problems solved, a **sample statistic**, could be scaled along the **Y-axis**. Note, however, that since a **frequency count** can also be gotten from the collected data, (the number of students solving 1, 2, ..., or 10 problems) number of problems can be represented along the **X-axis** with the frequency (number of students solving a specific number of problems) represented along the **Y-axis**. Since the number of problems solved is a **discrete quantitative variable**, a bar graph would be appropriate. In this case two bar graphs, one for each set of instructions, would be constructed. From these bar graphs you should be able to discern group patterns and determine whether the distribution is **symmetrical**, **positively skewed**, or **negatively skewed**.

Application Exercises

Chapter 4

1. Factors that influence our attitudes about a variety of
    things have always been of interest to social psychologists.
    One social psychologist interested in factors that influence
    attitudes measured the attitudes of college students as
    indicated by agreement with statements believed to be made
    by either a well-respected American politician or an
    infamous foreign terrorist. One hundred students were
    selected from an exceptionally large principles of
    psychology class by assigning a number to each student and
    having a computer generate a list of numbers to comprise the
    group such that each member of the class had an equally
    likely chance of being a member of the group. Agreement
    with statements such as *The pursuit of freedom is justified
    regardless of the means used to obtain it* was rated on a 5-
    point scale with 1 being *disagree strongly* and 5 being *agree
    strongly*. An average agreement score, rounded to the
    nearest whole number, was obtained for each student. A
    random half of the students were told that the statements
    were made by the well-respected American politician. The
    remaining half of the students were told the statements were
    made by the infamous foreign terrorist. An overall average
    score for each half of the students was calculated from the
    individual averages.

Identify

   a. the method of data collection (experimental,
       correlational, just frequency count).

   b. the group (sample or population) on which measures are
       taken.

   c. the type of sample(s) (random, randomized, biased), if
       appropriate.

   d. sample size(s), if appropriate.

   e. the independent variable, if appropriate.

   f. the dependent variable(s).

   g. the dependent measure(s).

   h. scale of measurement.

     i.   the type of measure (statistic or parameter) made on the group.

     j.   operational definition(s).

     k.   how the data should be organized in table format (give reason).

     l.   how the data should be organized in graph or display format (give reason).

     m.   the label for the *X*- and *Y*-axis for the graph(s) or the unit of measurement for the display(s).

2. Prejudice is a set of hostile attitudes about a particular group of persons. A social psychologist, who believes that an authoritarian personality characterized by unquestioning obedience to authority may be a contributing factor to prejudice, measures individuals' attitudes towards a variety of ethnic and religious groups using a rating scale devised for that purpose. The individuals' scores on an adjective check list which rates the degree to which an individual's personality type is authoritarian are also collected. High scores on this test indicate a high degree of authoritarianism. These data are collected from an entire group of nineteen students attending evening classes at a small community college in a rural area.

Identify

     a.   the method of data collection (experimental, correlational, just frequency count).

     b.   the group (sample or population) on which measures are taken.

c. the type of sample (random, randomized, biased), if appropriate.

d. sample size(s), if appropriate.

e. the independent variable, if appropriate.

f. the dependent variable(s).

g. the dependent measure(s).

h. scale of measurement.

i. the type of measure (statistic or parameter) made on the group.

j. operational definition(s).

k. how the data should be organized in table format (give reason).

l. how the data should be organized in graph or display format (give reason).

m. the label for the X- and Y-axis for the graph(s) or the unit of measurement for the display(s).

Chapter 4

MEETING THE CHALLENGE OF STATISTICS

The following problems pertain to the memory experiment described in the *Meeting the Challenge of Statistics* section in Chapter 1, pages 9-10. The number of syllables or words correctly recalled by the freshmen in each set of experimental and control groups reproduced from Chapter 1 are as follows:

Nonsense Syllables
Experimental: 12, 13, 11, 11, 9, 10, 13, 12, 12, 10
Control: 10, 11, 9, 9, 6, 11, 6, 5, 8, 8

Emotionally Neutral Words
Experimental: 12, 14, 13, 10, 14, 15, 11, 13, 16, 15
Control: 10, 11, 12, 8, 9, 9, 9, 8, 11, 9

Emotion Laden Words (pleasant, **unpleasant)**
Experimental: (9,**6)**, (10,8), (9,**7)**, (8,8), (7,6), (9,7), (10,**6)**,
(8,**5)**, (7,8), (9,**9)**
Control: (7,**5)**, (9,**5)**, (6,**5)**, (7,**6)**, (8,7), (7,**7)**, (6,7), (9,**4)**,
(6,**5)**, (5,7) .

1. In the space provided on the next page, construct a frequency polygon for the grouped frequency distribution in Table 4.1 which is the answer to problem 6, page 42, of this section in Chapter 3.

   Table 4.1
   Grouped Frequency Distribution of Recall Scores Presented in the *Meeting the Challenge of Statistics* Section of Chapter 1 with the Designated Criteria of $i = 2$ and $k = 8$

Class Interval	Frequency (f)
18 – 19	2
16 – 17	5
14 – 15	9
12 – 13	16
10 – 11	14
8 – 9	11
6 – 7	2
4 – 5	1
	$\Sigma = 60$

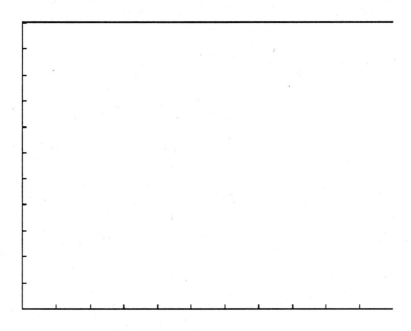

2. Construct a histogram for the grouped frequency distribution of Table 4.1 in problem 1.

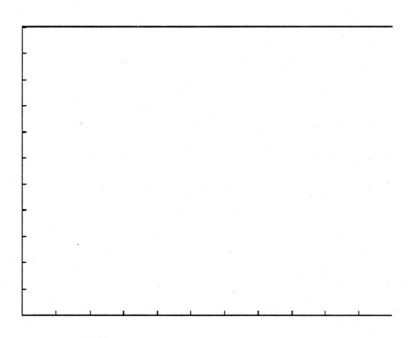

3. If averages of the experimental and control subgroups presented the list of emotionally neutral words were to be compared with the averages of the experimental and control subgroups from the other two groups of 20 freshmen, specify the type of graph that should be used.

4. Give the reason for your choice in problem 3.

5. Tell how you would depict the relationship between how well freshmen in the emotion laden group performed on the test of recall of emotionally pleasant words and how well they performed on the test of recall of emotionally unpleasant words.

6. Explain why it would be feasible or unfeasible to organize the data from the entire group of sixty freshmen as a stem-and-leaf display.

7. If the independent variable in the memory experiment had been duration of sleep instead of the three different types of learning events, how would the averages of the three experimental groups best be depicted graphically?

8. Give the reason for your choice in problem 7.

CHAPTER 5
MEASURES OF CENTRAL TENDENCY

DETAILED TEXTBOOK OUTLINE

Mode (Page 98)

Median (Page 100)

Mean (Page 103)

KEY TERMS AND DEFINITIONS

defining equation   The symbolic expression of an operational definition.

Mdn A designation for the median.

mean or arithmetic average The point in a distribution about which the sum of the deviations equals zero.

measures of central tendency Scores or points toward the center of the distribution that typify the scores in the distribution.

median The point in a distribution at or below which 50% of the scores fall.

midrange The point halfway between the highest and lowest score.

mode The score or measure that occurs most often in a distribution. For a grouped frequency distribution, it is the midpoint of the interval with the greatest frequency.

μ (pronounced "mu") Symbol for the mean of a population.

multimodal distributions Distributions in which the frequencies cluster around two or more nonadjacent scores or class intervals.

P_{50} The fiftieth percentile; another expression for the median.

$P_{50} = LRL_p + i([n_{bp} - n_{LRL}])/f$ A computational formula for the median.

raw score deviation A deviation of a score from the mean in raw score units.

sampling stability A reference to the extent that repeated sampling will lead to the same outcome.

statistical versatility Reference to the many uses of a statistic. A summary statistic that is versatile can be used for description, in other statistical derivations, and in statistical inference.

summary statistic A sample measure that in some way summarizes or typifies a distribution.

$\Sigma(X - \bar{X}) = 0$ Defining equation for the mean.

unbiased estimate A statistic that on the average equals the corresponding population parameter.

$\bar{X}$ (pronounced X-bar) The symbol for the mean of a sample.

$\bar{X} = \Sigma X/N$ The computational formula for the mean of raw data or an array.

Chapter 5

$\bar{X} = \Sigma fX / \Sigma f$ The computational formula for the mean of a
   frequency distribution. For grouped frequency
   distributions, X refers to the midpoint (X') of the class
   interval.

MASTERING THE LANGUAGE OF STATISTICS

Fill-in-the-Blanks

Write the appropriate term(s) in the space(s) provided.

Oftentimes, instead of presenting data in table, graph or

display format, an investigator may wish to present a single

score or measure that in some way represents the characteristic

of interest or typifies the scores in a distribution. Such

measures or scores are called _____ statistics. Summary

statistics that tend to be towards the center of a distribution

are called measures of _____ _____. The _____ is

the easiest measure of _____ _____ to obtain and is

most often used when the measure of the sample characteristic or

dependent variable is either normally or inherently discrete.

The _____ is a score or measure that occurs most often. In a

_____ frequency distribution, it is the score with the

greatest frequency. In a _____ frequency distribution, it

is the midpoint of the interval with the greatest frequency.

One serious limitation of the _____ as a measure of central

tendency is that it need not occur. A second limitation of the

_____ is that there may be more than one. Distributions with

more than one mode are called _____ distributions. A

third limitation of the mode is that it lacks sampling

_____. Sampling _____ refers to the extent that

repeated sampling would lead to the same outcome. The mode also lacks statistical _____. Statistical _____ refers to the many uses of a summary statistic. A _____ statistic that is _____ can be used for description, in other statistical derivations, and in statistical inference.

Another measure of _____ _____ that is frequently used for skewed distributions is the _____. The _____, denoted *Mdn*, is the point in a distribution at or below which 50% of the cases fall. Accordingly, it is also called the _____th percentile and symbolized_____. Although median implies middle, it is not the point halfway between the highest and lowest score. That point is called the _____. The _____ is the halfway point only with respect to the *number of scores* falling on each side of it. The median has greater statistical _____ than the mode since it is used in statistical formulas that permit you to make inferences about the shapes of populations. The computational formula for the median of a frequency distribution is _____.

Another summary measure that typifies a distribution is called the _____ or arithmetic average. The _____ or arithmetic average is symbolized _____ and is operationally defined as the point in a distribution about which the sum of the raw score deviations equals zero. A _____ _____ _____ is a distance from the mean in raw score units. Thus, the _____ equation for the mean is expressed _____. A _____ equation is the symbolic expression of an operational definition. The _____ for a data set can be obtained by dividing the sum of all the scores (symbolized _____) by the number of scores (symbolized _____). Thus, the computational formula for the mean is expressed _____. When the mean is computed for a simple frequency distribution the formula is expressed _____. When the mean is computed for a grouped frequency distribution, the X in the formula $\bar{X} = \Sigma fX/\Sigma f$ refers to the _____ of the class interval. The mean of a random _____ is a(n) _____ estimate of its population _____, μ.

True-False Items

Place a T for true or an F for false in the space provided before each item.

1. _____ The point in a distribution at or below which 50% of the cases fall is called the median.

2. _____ A distribution can have more than one mode.

3. _____ The mode is the most appropriate measure of central tendency when the characteristic of interest or dependent variable is normally or inherently discrete.

4. _____ The median is the point in a distribution about which the sum of the deviations equals zero.

5. _____ Statistical versatility refers to the extent that repeated sampling will lead to different outcomes.

6. _____ A biased estimate of a population parameter is a statistic that on the average does not equal its corresponding population parameter.

7. _____ The symbolic expression of an operational definition is called a computational formula.

8. _____ Both *Mdn* and P_{50} are ways of designating the mean.

9. _____ Distributions in which frequencies cluster around two or more adjacent scores or class intervals are called multimodal distributions.

10. _____ Sampling stability refers to the many uses of a statistic.

11.____ The formula $\bar{X} = \Sigma X/N$ is the formula for obtaining the mean of raw data or an array.

12.____ The midrange is the point halfway between the highest and lowest score.

Multiple-Choice Items

Blacken out the letter corresponding to the correct answer.

1. The measure of central tendency most appropriate for skewed distributions is the
   (a) mode.
   (b) median.
   (c) mean.
   (d) midrange.

2. A symbol for the mean is
   (a) *Mdn*.
   (b) $\bar{X}$.
   (c) P_{50}.
   (d) all of the above.

3. A distribution may have more than one
   (a) mode.
   (b) median.
   (c) mean.
   (d) midrange.

4. An unbiased estimate of the population parameter, μ, is the
   (a) mode.
   (b) median.
   (c) mean.
   (d) midrange.

5. The most versatile measure of central tendency is the
   (a) mode.
   (b) median.
   (c) mean.
   (d) midrange.

6. A reference to the extent that repeated sampling will lead to the same outcome is called
   (a) statistical versatility.
   (b) unbiased estimate.
   (c) statistical stability.
   (d) central tendency.

7. The formula $\bar{X} = \Sigma fX'/\Sigma f$ is the computational formula for the mean of
   (a) raw data.
   (b) an array.
   (c) a simple frequency distribution.
   (d) a grouped frequency distribution.

8. If a distribution is skewed to the right, then
   (a) the median is usually larger than the mean.
   (b) the mean is usually larger than the mode.
   (c) the mode is usually larger than the median.
   (d) the mode is usually between the mean and the median.

9. In selecting a measure of central tendency which of the following is of little concern?
   (a) the type of variable
   (b) the sample size
   (c) the shape of the distribution
   (d) the scale of measurement

10. Which measure of central tendency is sensitive to each and every score?
    (a) mode
    (b) median
    (c) mean
    (d) midrange

11. Which measure of central tendency would best represent the scores on a very difficult psychology exam?
    (a) mode
    (b) mean
    (c) midrange
    (d) median

12. Which measure of central tendency would best represent the typical size of an American family?
    (a) mean
    (b) median
    (c) mode
    (d) midrange

APPLYING STATISTICAL CONCEPTS

Example Application

The following data represent the study time (hours per week) of fifty students who were on academic probation during the first term of their sophomore year in college:

20, 34, 48, 19, 24, 27, 17, 21, 29, 23, 17, 27, 34, 39, 22, 24,
21, 23, 44, 42, 40, 12, 24, 41, 38, 22, 24, 20, 20, 23, 25, 31,
32, 33, 26, 34, 36, 37, 39, 19, 25, 22, 21, 27, 34, 32, 29, 21,
22, 29.

If you perform the arithmetic operations and apply the formulas described in Chapter 5 of your textbook to these **raw scores**, you find that the sum of these scores divided by the number of scores, $\Sigma X/N$, equals 27.66 (1383/50), the **mean** of this **data set**. If you organize these data into an **array** you can by inspection readily determine that the score that occurs most often, the **mode**, is 24. You can also by inspection and a simple arithmetic operation, (25 + 26)/2, determine that the **median**, the point at or below which 50% of the scores fall is 25.5. You should realize that you will also obtain these values for these three **measures of central tendency** if the data set is organized into a **simple frequency distribution**. However, if the data are organized into a grouped frequency distribution such as that shown in Table 5.1, the values may differ slightly.

Table 5.1
The Amount of Study Time (Hours per Week) for Students on Academic Probation during the First Semester of Their Sophomore Year in College (N = 50)

Class Interval	Tally Marks	Frequency f	Midpoint X'	Transformed Midpoint (X''')	fX'''
42 – 44	//	2	43	5	10
39 – 41	////	4	40	4	16
36 – 38	////	4	37	3	12
33 – 35	/////	5	34	2	10
30 – 32	///	3	31	1	3
27 – 29	//////	6	28	0	0
24 – 26	///////	7	25	−1	−7
21 – 23	///////////	11	22	−2	−22
18 – 20	/////	5	19	−3	−15
15 – 17	//	2	16	−4	−8
12 – 14	/	1	13	−5	−5
	Σf =	50		$\Sigma fX'''$ =	−.12

Using the **midpoints** (X') the **mean** is computed to be 27.64, (13892/50), a value very close to that obtained for the raw scores. Of course, the same value is obtained when the transformed scores are used, −.12(3) + 28 = 27.64. The **mode**, however, is found to be 22 instead of the 24, the raw score that occurred most often. Using the formula $P_{50} = LRL_p + i([n_{bp} - n_{LRL}])/f$ the value calculated for the median is 23.5 + 3([25 − 19])/7 = 26.07, a value slightly larger than that obtained from the raw scores.

By examining the three **measures of central tendency** or by putting the data into a graph format, a **frequency polygon**, you can tell that the points tend to cluster around the low values and trail off away from the intersection or zero point of the *X*- and *Y*-axis and the distribution, therefore, is skewed to the right or **positively skewed**.

Application Exercises

1. Systematic desensitization is a behavior therapy that is often used with individuals suffering from a phobia, an inordinate, irrational fear of some specific object or event. An investigator wishes to determine how many sessions in general are required to cure individuals of fear of flying in an airplane. A number of behavior therapists are asked to report the number of sessions required to cure their patients of a flying phobia. A cure meant the person could fly in an airplane and report that they experienced no fear of flying. The following are the number of sessions needed to cure patients of a flying phobia that were reported to the investigator by the behavior therapists: 10, 13, 12, 10, 13, 14, 11, 10, 11, 10, 12, 11, 13, 12, 9, 15, 10, 11, 10, 14, 17, 10, 9, 10, 11.

    Specify

    a. the population.

    b. whether the group on which the measures were taken constitutes the population or a sample.

    c. whether the sample is random, randomized, or biased.

    d. the scale of measurement.

    e. any operational definition(s).

    f. the range of the raw scores.

    g. the mean of the raw scores.

    h. the mode of the raw scores.

    i. the median of the raw scores.

    j. the most appropriate measure of central tendency.

    k. the most appropriate table format.

    l. the reason for your answer to part *j*.

    m. the most appropriate graph to depict the data.

    n. the most probable shape of the frequency distribution.

    o. the effect multiplying each score by 6 has on the mean.

2. Suppose you were read a series of numbers, for example a nine number zip code, that you were supposed to remember after a single reading. How many of the numbers could you recall? The number of items, in this example *numbers*, that can be recalled after a single presentation is called "memory span." A developmental psychologist wants to determine the memory span of eight-year-old children from a local school. The superintendent of the school gives the psychologist permission to test the memory span of eight-year-olds under his supervision. The psychologist writes the name of each eight-year-old at the school on a slip of paper, puts the papers into a box, mixes them thoroughly, and withdraws 20 of them one at a time. The psychologist tests the memory span of these twenty children with the following results: 7, 5, 8, 7, 7, 9, 8, 9, 7, 6, 7, 6, 5, 7, 6, 6, 7, 8, 7, 8.

   Specify

   a. the population.

b. whether the group on which the measures were taken constitutes the population or a sample.

c. whether the sample is random, randomized, or biased.

d. the scale of measurement.

e. any operational definition(s).

f. the range of the raw scores.

g. the mean of the raw scores.

h. the mode of the raw scores.

i. the median of the raw scores.

j. the most appropriate measure of central tendency.

k. the most appropriate table format.

l. the reason for your answer to part *j*.

m. the most appropriate graph to depict the data.

n. the most probable shape of the frequency distribution.

o. the effect multiplying each score by 6 has on the mean.

Chapter 5

MEETING THE CHALLENGE OF STATISTICS

The following problems pertain to the memory experiment described in the *Meeting the Challenge of Statistics* section in Chapter 1, pages 9-10. The number of syllables or words correctly recalled by the freshmen in each set of experimental and control groups reproduced from Chapter 1 are as follows:

Nonsense Syllables
Experimental: 12, 13, 11, 11, 9, 10, 13, 12, 12, 10
Control: 10, 11, 9, 9, 6, 11, 6, 5, 8, 8

Emotionally Neutral Words
Experimental: 12, 14, 13, 10, 14, 15, 11, 13, 16, 15
Control: 10, 11, 12, 8, 9, 9, 9, 8, 11, 9

Emotion Laden Words (pleasant, **unpleasant)**
Experimental: (9,6), (10,8), (9,7), (8,8), (7,6), (9,7), (10,6), (8,5), (7,8), (9,9)
Control: (7,5), (9,5), (6,5), (7,6), (8,7), (7,7), (6,7), (9,4), (6,5), (5,7)

1. Compute the mean number of words recalled by the experimental and control groups that were presented emotionally neutral words.

2. Determine the modal number of words recalled by the experimental group presented emotion laden words.

3. Determine the median number of words recalled by the control group presented nonsense syllables.

4. Compute the mode, mean, and median of the grouped frequency distribution in Table 5.2, which is the answer to problem 6, page 42, in Chapter 3.

Table 5.2
Grouped Frequency Distribution of Recall Scores Presented in the *Meeting the Challenge of Statistics* Section of Chapter 1 with the Designated Criteria of $i = 2$ and $k = 8$

Class Interval	Frequency (f)
18 – 19	2
16 – 17	5
14 – 15	9
12 – 13	16
10 – 11	14
8 – 9	11
6 – 7	2
4 – 5	1
	$\Sigma = 60$

5. On the basis of the values for the mode, mean, and median in problem 4, determine the shape (symmetrical, negatively skewed, positively skewed) of the distribution in Table 5.2.

6. Using transformed scores, compute the mean of the distribution in Table 5.3, which is the answer to problem 8, page 43, in Chapter 3.

Table 5.3
Grouped Frequency Distribution of Recall Scores Presented in the *Meeting the Challenge of Statistics* Section of Chapter 1 with the Designated Criteria of $i = 2$ and $k = 7$

Class Interval	Frequency (f)
17–18	2
15–16	10
13–14	13
11–12	16
9–10	12
7– 8	4
5– 6	3
	$\Sigma = 60$

7. Determine the midrange from the raw scores of the entire sample of freshmen.

8. Organize the data from the control group presented nonsense syllables as a simple frequency distribution and compute the mean of the distribution.

CHAPTER 6
MEASURES OF DISPERSION

DETAILED TEXTBOOK OUTLINE

Chapter 6

KEY TERMS AND DEFINITIONS

absolute value of a score The value of a score irrespective of its sign.

average deviation An average of the absolute values of the raw score deviations from the mean.

between-group variance The variance of the means of groups of individuals.

between-subject variance The variance of the means of the individuals of a group.

degrees of freedom The number of scores in a sample that are free to vary.

df Symbol for degrees of freedom.

first quartile A summary statistic that marks off the lower 25% of the scores of a distribution.

interquartile range The distance between the first and third quartiles.

measure of dispersion A summary statistic that describes how dispersed or spread out scores in a distribution are or how variable a distribution is.

population variance Refers to the average of the squared raw score deviations from the population mean.

Q_1 Symbol for the first quartile, a summary statistic that marks off the lower 25% of the scores of a distribution.

Q_3 Symbol for the third quartile, a summary statistic that marks off the upper 25% of the scores of a distribution.

quartile deviation Half of the interquartile range; also called the semi-interquartile range.

s Symbol for the standard deviation of a sample.

$s = \sqrt{[\Sigma X^2 - (\Sigma X)^2 / N] / (N-1)}$ Computational formula for the standard deviation.

s^2 Symbol for the sample variance.

$s^2 = [\Sigma X^2 - (\Sigma X)^2 / N] / (N - 1)$ Computational formula for the sample variance that is an unbiased estimate of the population variance, σ^2.

Chapter 6

$s^2 = [\Sigma fX^2 - (\Sigma fX)^2/\Sigma f]/(\Sigma f - 1)$ Computational formula for the sample variance of frequency distributions.

sample variance   An adjusted average of the squared raw score deviations from the sample mean, that is, the sum of the raw score deviations from the sample mean divided by the degrees of freedom.

semi-interquartile range or **quartile deviation,** $Q_3 - Q_1/2$ Half of the interquartile range.

σ^2 (Pronounced "sigma squared") A symbol for the population variance.

standard deviation   An adjusted average raw score deviation; the square root of the variance.

third quartile   A summary statistic that marks off the upper 25% of the scores of a distribution.

within-group variance   Variance of the scores within a group.

within-subject variance Variance of an individual's scores.

MASTERING THE LANGUAGE OF STATISTICS

Full-in-the-Blanks

Write the appropriate term(s) in the spaces(s) provided.

In the previous chapter we focused on the mean, median, and mode, measures of _____ _____. In this chapter we focus on measures of _____, summary statistics that describe how spread out a distribution is. You encountered a measure of dispersion in Chapter 3 of the textbook and this workbook called the _____ of the raw scores. The _____ is the distance between the upper real limit of the highest score and the lower real limit of the lowest score. A range statistic that is not as sensitive to extreme scores as the range is called the _____ range, the distance between the first and third quartiles. The _____ _____ is a point that marks off the lower 25% of the scores. The _____

_____ is a point that marks off the upper 25% of the

scores. Half of the distance between the first and third

quartiles is called the _____ _____ _____.

Another name for the semi-interquartile range is the _____

_____.

A _____ score as you recall from the previous chapter

refers to a score's distance from the mean. The _____ value

of a score's distance from the mean is its value irrespective of

its sign. The average of the absolute values of the raw score

deviations from the mean is called the _____ deviation and

is also a measure of _____. The _____ deviation,

like the range statistics, is not statistically _____

because it is used for little more than a descriptive purpose.

An adjusted average of the squared raw score deviations from the

mean, called the _____ _____ is, however,

statistically versatile, since it is used not only for a

descriptive purpose but also to derive other statistics and is

used in statistical inference. The population _____,

symbolized _____, is a parameter. The sample variance,

symbolized _____, is a _____ and a(n) _____

estimate of the population _____. The sample variance is

operationally defined as the sum of the squared raw score

deviations from the mean divided by the degrees of _____.

Degrees of freedom is symbolized _____ and refers to the number

of scores that are free to vary. The defining equation for the

variance then could be expressed as _____.

Chapter 6

The square root of the sample variance is called the _____

_____. The standard deviation, symbolized ____, is a

commonly used measure of dispersion for distributions for which

the mean is the most appropriate measure of _____

_____. The computational formula for the standard

deviation of raw data or an array is _____. For a

simple frequency distribution this formula translates into

_____.

The variance of certain types of scores or measures are

given special names. For example, the variance of a set of

scores for a single individual is referred to as _____-

_____ variance. In contrast, the variance of the means of

the scores for several subjects is referred to as _____-

_____ variance. Similarly, the variance of the scores for a

group of subjects is called _____-_____ variance, and

the variance of the means of groups of individuals is called

_____-_____ variance.

True-False Items

*Place a T for true or an F for false in the space provided
before each item.*

1.____ Another name for the interquartile range is the quartile
deviation.

2.____ The average deviation, interquartile range, and variance
are measures of dispersion.

3.____ The average of the squared raw score deviations from the
population mean is the average deviation.

4.____ The standard deviation is the square root of the
variance.

5.____ s^2 is the symbol for the population variance.

Chapter 6

6.____ Half of the interquartile range is called the semi-interquartile range.

7.____ A summary statistic that marks off the upper 25% of the scores of a distribution is called the third quartile.

8.____ Q_1 is the symbol for the summary statistic that marks off the lower 25% of the scores of a distribution.

9.____ The symbol *df* represents the number of scores that are not free to vary.

10.____ The variance of the means of the individuals of a group is called between-subject variance.

11.____ The variance of the scores within a group of individuals is called within-subject variance.

12.____ The sum of the raw score deviations from the mean divided by the number of scores that are free to vary is called the sample variance.

Multiple-Choice Items

Blacken out the letter corresponding to the correct answer.

1. The value of a score irrespective of its sign is called
   (a) a raw score.
   (b) a transformed score.
   (c) the absolute value of the score.
   (d) a score that is free to vary.

2. Half the distance between the first and third quartiles is called the
   (a) interquartile range.
   (b) quartile deviation.
   (c) absolute value.
   (d) standard deviation.

3. The semi-interquartile range is another name for the
   (a) standard deviation.
   (b) sample variance
   (c) quartile deviation.
   (d) average deviation.

4. A summary statistic that marks off the upper 25% of the distribution is the
   (a) quartile deviation.
   (b) interquartile range.
   (c) third quartile.
   (d) 25th percentile.

5. The variance of scores within a group of individuals is called
   (a) between-group variance.
   (b) within-group variance.
   (c) between-subject variance.
   (d) within-subject variance.

6. An adjusted average of the squared raw score deviations from the sample mean is the
   (a) sample standard deviation.
   (b) unbiased estimate of the population variance.
   (c) population variance.
   (d) average deviation.

7. The average of the absolute values of the raw score deviations from the mean is the
   (a) standard deviation.
   (b) raw score deviation.
   (c) average deviation.
   (d) quartile deviation.

8. The variance of an individual's scores is the
   (a) between-subject variance.
   (b) within-subject variance.
   (c) within-group variance.
   (d) population variance.

9. The symbol for the population variance is
   (a) σ.
   (b) Q_{25}.
   (c) s.
   (d) none of the above.

10. The symbol for the sample variance is
    (a) s^2.
    (b) σ^2.
    (c) Q_{25}.
    (d) μ.

11. A summary statistic that describes how spread out scores in a distribution are is called
    (a) the range.
    (b) a measure of dispersion.
    (c) the variance.
    (d) all of the above.

12. The square root of the variance is called the
    (a) quartile deviation.
    (b) raw score deviation.
    (c) standard deviation.
    (d) average deviation.

Chapter 6

APPLYING STATISTICAL CONCEPTS

Example Application

The times to the nearest second it takes 30 rats in a learning experiment to traverse a complex maze on an errorless run through the maze are: 37, 35, 33, 32, 30, 30, 29, 28, 28, 27, 26, 24, 24, 24, 24, 23, 23, 23, 23, 21, 20, 18, 18, 18, 17, 16, 15, 14, 13, 11.

If you apply what you have learned in this and the preceding chapters you can tell by inspection that the data are organized as **an array**, that the **range, a measure of dispersion**, equals 27, and that the **mode** and **median** are 23.5. Because the mode and median are equal, the distribution is probably **symmetrical** and the **mean**, therefore, would also be equal to 23.5. Applying the formula for the mean $\bar{X} = \Sigma X/N$ indicates that the mean does equal 23.5 (703/30 = 23.5).

Applying the formula for the **sample variance** computed from an array, you find $s^2 = [\Sigma X^2 - (\Sigma X)^2/N]/(N - 1) = [17,810 - (704)^2/30]/(30-1) = 44.46$. This sample variance is **within-group variance** and is an **unbiased estimate** of the **population variance**, σ^2. The square root of the sample variance, the **standard deviation**, equals 6.67. The sample size minus 1 (N - 1) in the formula for s^2 is called the **degrees of freedom**. The symbol for degrees of freedom is **df**.

The maze learning data are organized in Table 6.1 as a **grouped frequency distribution** with i = 3 and k = 10.

Table 6.1
A Grouped Frequency Distribution of the Time to the Nearest Second it Takes Rats in a Learning Experiment to Traverse a Complex Maze on an Errorless Run through the Maze (N = 30)

Class Interval	f	X'	X'''	X^2'''	fX'''	fX^2'''
36 – 38	1	37	5	25	5	25
33 – 35	2	34	4	16	8	32
30 – 32	3	31	3	9	9	27
27 – 29	4	28	2	4	8	16
24 – 26	5	25	1	1	5	5
21 – 23	5	22	0	0	0	0
18 – 20	4	19	-1	1	-4	4
15 – 17	3	16	-2	4	-6	12
12 – 14	2	13	-3	9	-6	18
09 – 11	1	10	-4	16	-4	16
	30				15	155

The formula for computing the variance of frequency distributions is applied to the transformed scores in Table 6.1

Chapter 6

as follows: $s^2 = [\Sigma fX^2 - (\Sigma fX)^2/\Sigma f]/(\Sigma f - 1) = [155 -
(15)^2/30]/(30 - 1) = 5.09$. Converting the variance of the
transformed scores to the variance of the original distribution
requires multiplying s^2 by i^2. The variance of the original
distribution is, therefore, 5.09 X 9 = 45.81. Again, note that
measures computed from a grouped frequency distribution may not
be the same as those computed from the **raw scores**.

Application Exercises

1. Goslings generally become attached to a moving object that
   they see and follow within a short period of time after
   hatching from the egg. This attachment behavior is called
   imprinting. The probability of obtaining successful
   imprinting in the laboratory increases following hatching
   to some optimal age level and then declines. Table 6.2 is a
   frequency distribution of the number of Greylag Goslings
   that imprinted to a moving toy train in the laboratory at
   various times after hatching from the egg.

   Table 6.2
   A Grouped Frequency Distribution of the Number of Greylag
   Goslings Successfully Imprinting in the Laboratory at
   Various Hours after Hatching from the Egg ($N = 70$)

Class Interval (Hours)	Frequency (f)	Transformed Midpoint (X''')
30 – 32	2	5
27 – 29	3	4
24 – 26	5	3
21 – 23	7	2
18 – 20	10	1
15 – 17	15	0
12 – 14	9	-1
09 – 11	8	-2
06 – 08	6	-3
03 – 05	4	-4
00 – 02	1	-5

   For the data organized in Table 6.2, determine

   a. the midpoint of the class interval 15 – 17.

   b. the width of the class intervals.

c. the mean of the distribution using the transformed scores.

d. the mode of the distribution.

e. the median of the distribution.

f. the range of the distribution.

g. the sample variance using the transformed scores.

h. the standard deviation.

i. the name of the most appropriate graph.

j. the degrees of freedom.

k. the type of variance in part *g*.

2. In a classical conditioning experiment, a response such as salivation comes to be elicited by a stimulus, for example a tone, which at the outset of the experiment did not elicit the response. The response occurs as a result of the stimulus (in this case a tone) being repeatedly paired with a stimulus such as food which does elicit the response of salivation. The following is the number of pairings needed before the tone elicited the response of salivation by 12 experimental subjects: 9, 9, 8, 11, 10, 15, 9, 10, 9, 16, 7, 7.

Determine

a. the form in which the data are presented (for example an array).

b. an array in table format with column headings and values for X, X^2, and $|X - \bar{X}|$.

c. the most appropriate way to present the average graphically, if appropriate.

d. values for three measures of central tendency.

e. the range of the scores.

f. the average deviation.

g. Q_1 and Q_3.

h. the interquartile range.

i. the quartile deviation.

    j. an unbiased estimate of the population variance.

    k. the standard deviation.

MEETING THE CHALLENGE OF STATISTICS

The following problems pertain to the memory experiment described in the *Meeting the Challenge of Statistics* section in Chapter 1, pages 9-10, and the answers to that section in Chapter 3 of this workbook.

The following are the number of syllables or words correctly recalled by the freshmen in each set of experimental and control groups:

Nonsense Syllables
Experimental: 12, 13, 11, 11, 9, 10, 13, 12, 12, 10
Control: 10, 11, 9, 9, 6, 11, 6, 5, 8, 8

Emotionally Neutral Words
Experimental: 12, 14, 13, 10, 14, 15, 11, 13, 16, 15
Control: 10, 11, 12, 8, 9, 9, 9, 8, 11, 9

Emotion Laden Words (pleasant, **unpleasant)**
Experimental: (9,**6**), (10,**8**), (9,**7**), (8,**8**), (7,**6**), (9,**7**), (10,**6**), (8,**5**), (7,**8**), (9,**9)**
Control: (7,**5**), (9,**5**), (6,**5**), (7,**6**), (8,**7**), (7,**7**), (6,**7**), (9,**4**), (6,**5**), (5,**7**)

1. Compute the average deviation for the experimental group presented emotionally neutral words.

2. Determine the range of the scores for the control group presented emotion laden words.

3. Compute (a) Q_1 and Q_3, (b) the interquartile range, and (c) the quartile deviation for the raw scores of the 20 subjects presented nonsense syllables.

4. Compute (a) the variance and (b) standard deviation for the control group presented emotionally neutral words.

5. Using midpoints (X'), compute (a) the variance and (b) the standard deviation of the grouped frequency distribution in Table 6.3 which is the answer to problem 6 of this section in Chapter 3.

Table 6.3
Grouped Frequency Distribution of Recall Scores Presented in the *Meeting the Challenge of Statistics* Section of Chapter 1 with the Designated Criteria of $i = 2$ and $k = 8$

Class Interval	Frequency	
18 – 19	2	
16 – 17	5	
14 – 15	9	
12 – 13	16	
10 – 11	14	
8 – 9	11	
6 – 7	2	
4 – 5	1	
	$\Sigma = 60$	

6. Compute an unbiased estimate of the variance of the population from which the twenty subjects presented nonsense syllables were assumed to be selected.

7. Using scores transformed by subtraction of a central midpoint and division by the class interval width, compute (a) the variance and (b) the standard deviation of the distribution in Table 6.4 which is the answer to problem 8 of this section in Chapter 3.

Table 6.4
Grouped Frequency Distribution of Recall Scores Presented in Meeting the Challenge of Statistics Section of Chapter 1 with the Designated Criteria of $i = 2$ and $k = 7$

Class Interval Frequency (f)

Class Interval	Frequency (f)
17–18	2
15–16	10
13–14	13
11–12	16
9–10	12
7– 8	4
5– 6	3
	$\Sigma = 60$

8. Compute (a) the variance and (b) the standard deviation of the simple frequency distribution in Table 6.5 which is the answer to problem 8 of this section in Chapter 5.

Table 6.5
Simple Frequency Distribution of Number of Syllables
<u>Recalled by Control Group Subjects Presented Nonsense</u>
<u>Syllables</u>

Syllables Recalled	Frequency (f)
11	2
10	1
9	2
8	2
7	0
6	2
5	1
	$\Sigma = 10$

CHAPTER 7
MEASURES OF RELATIVE STANDING

DETAILED TEXTBOOK OUTLINE

Chapter 7

KEY TERMS AND DEFINITIONS

decile A quantile designation for values that divide the area under a frequency polygon into ten equal parts.

percentile A quantile designation for values that divide the area under a frequency polygon into one hundred equal parts and is a point in a distribution at or below which a specified percentage of the cases fall.

percentile rank The percentile rank of a score is a value indicating the percentage of cases falling at or below that score.

P_k Symbol for percentile where k takes on values from 1 to 99.

quantiles The collective name for values such as deciles, percentiles, and quartiles that divide a frequency distribution into a specified number of groups with equal frequencies.

standard or z-score The distance of a raw score from the mean in standard deviation units.

$X = zs + \bar{X}$ Formula for transforming a z-score to a raw score.

z Symbol for a standard score or z-score.

z-score The distance of a raw score from the mean in standard deviation units.

$z = (X - \bar{X})/s$ Defining equation for a standard score or z-score.

MASTERING THE LANGUAGE OF STATISTICS

Fill-in-the-Blanks

Write the appropriate term(s) in the space(s) provided.

This chapter is concerned with procedures used to obtain measures of relative standing such as _____ _____, a value indicating the percentage of cases falling at or below a score. The _____ _____ of a score can be estimated graphically or determined mathematically. The raw score associated with a particular percentile rank is called a

_____. A _____ is a point in a distribution

of scores at or below which a specified percentage of the scores

fall. Percentiles are symbolized _____ where k takes on values

from 1 to 99. Certain percentiles are given special

designations such as D_1 or Q_2. The Q refers to quartile and the

D refers to _____. Percentiles, quartiles, and deciles

are collectively called _____. The _____, like

percentile rank, can be estimated graphically or determined

mathematically.

Another measure of relative standing is called a

_____ score. A _____ score indicates how far a raw

score is from the mean in standard deviation units. A standard

score symbolized by z is also referred to as a _____.

The formula for converting a raw score to a z-score is

_____. A z-score can be converted to a raw score by

applying the formula $X =$ _____.

True-False Items

*Place a T for true or an F for false in the space provided
before each item.*

1. ____ The percentile rank of a score is a value indicating the
   number of cases falling at or below the score.

2. ____ A percentile is a point in a distribution at or below
   which a specified percentage of the scores fall.

3. ____ Quantiles are symbolized Q_k.

4. ____ The deciles divide the area under a frequency polygon
   into ten equal parts.

5. ____ The quartiles divide the area of a frequency polygon
   into twenty-five equal parts.

6.____ Collectively, percentiles, deciles, and quartiles are referred to as quantiles.

7.____ Percentiles divide the area of a frequency polygon into 100 equal parts.

8.____ The quantiles P_{50}, D_5, and Q_2 refer to the same point in a distribution.

9.____ A standard score indicates how far a raw score is from the mean in standard deviation units.

10.____ The standard score symbolized by z is also called a z-score.

11.____ The formula $z = (\bar{X} - X)/s$ is used to transform a raw score to a z-score.

12.____ The formula $X = zs + \bar{X}$ is used to transform a z-score to a raw score.

Multiple-Choice Items

Blacken out the letter corresponding to the correct answer.

1. A percentile rank of a score is
   (a) a value indicating the percentage of cases falling at or below the given score.
   (b) a value indicating the number of cases falling at or below the given score.
   (c) a point in a distribution at or below which a specified number of the cases fall.
   (d) a point in a distribution at or below which a specified percentage of the cases fall.

2. A percentile is
   (a) a value indicating the number of cases falling at or below a given score.
   (b) a point in the distribution at or below which a specified percentage of the scores fall.
   (c) a value indicating the percentage of cases falling at or below a given score.
   (d) a point in the distribution at or below which a specified number of the cases fall.

3. In addition to *Mdn* another way to designate the median is
   (a) P_{50}.
   (b) Q_2.
   (c) D_5.
   (d) all of the above.

4. Collectively, percentiles and deciles are referred to as
   (a) ranks.
   (b) measures of central tendency.
   (c) quartiles.
   (d) quantiles.

5. Another designation for the point Q_3 is
   (a) P_{30}.
   (b) D_3.
   (c) P_{75}.
   (d) none of the above.

6. Quartiles divide the area of a frequency polygon into
   (a) twenty-five equal parts.
   (b) four equal parts.
   (c) ten equal parts.
   (d) ninety-nine equal parts.

7. The collective name for values that divide a frequency distribution into a specified number of groups with equal frequencies is
   (a) percentiles.
   (b) deciles.
   (c) quartiles.
   (d) none of the above.

8. Percentiles divide a frequency distribution into _____ groups with equal frequencies.
   (a) 100
   (b) 99
   (c) 10
   (d) 4

9. A score that indicates how far a raw score is from the mean in standard deviation units is a
   (a) quantile.
   (b) z-score.
   (c) percentile rank.
   (d) percentile.

10. The formula for transforming a raw score to a standard score is
    (a) $X = zs + \bar{X}$.
    (b) $X = zs - \bar{X}$.
    (c) $z = (X - \bar{X})/s$.
    (d) $z = (X + \bar{X})/s$.

11. The formula for transforming a standard score to a raw score is
    (a) $X = zs + \bar{X}$.
    (b) $X = zs - \bar{X}$.
    (c) $z = (X - \bar{X})/s$.
    (d) $z = (X + \bar{X})/s$.

12. A plus (+) or minus (−) sign before a z-score indicates
    (a) the z-score is higher or lower than the raw score.
    (b) the position of the z-score relative to the mean.
    (c) the z-score should be added to or subtracted from the raw score.
    (d) all of the above.

APPLYING STATISTICAL CONCEPTS

Example Application

Cognitive dissonance is a state of discomfort brought about by two or more inconsistent beliefs, attitudes, or behaviors. For example, a person knows that smoking cigarettes causes heart disorders and yet the person smokes. Here, the belief (cigarette smoking causes heart disorders) is inconsistent with the person's behavior (smoking). A social psychologist interested in the way individuals reduce dissonance sets up situations in which people must behave in a way that is inconsistent with their beliefs or attitudes, such as doing a favor for someone they dislike. Each of 50 participants is subjected to 10 such situations. Later each participant's beliefs or attitudes are again assessed to determine the number of beliefs or attitudes that change as a result of engaging in the dissonant behaviors.

The same 50 individuals participate in a second study in which their attitudes or beliefs about 19 medical statements are assessed. The participants then hear medical experts' arguments against their attitudes or beliefs. Again their attitudes and beliefs about the medical statements are assessed to see how many have changed as a result of the arguments of the experts. The social psychologist wants to see if there is a relationship between self-persuasion (changing one's beliefs or attitudes as a result of cognitive dissonance) and persuasion by experts. The results of the two studies are shown in Table 7.1.

Table 7.1
Frequency Distributions of the Number of Attitudes or Beliefs
That Changed as a Result of Self-Persuasion and as a Result of
Persuasion by Medical Experts ($N = 50$)

Self Persuasion		Persuasion by Medical Experts	
Score (X)	f	Class Interval	f
10	2	18 – 19	4
9	3	16 – 17	4
8	4	14 – 15	5
7	6	12 – 13	5
6	7	10 – 11	7
5	8	08 – 09	7
4	10	06 – 07	8
3	7	04 – 05	5
2	2	02 – 03	3
1	1	00 – 01	2

The statistical procedures that you learned in this and
preceding chapters should allow you to determine for this
correlational design the **relative standing** of any of the
participants in these distributions in terms of both **percentile
rank** and **standard** or **z-scores**. You should be able to convert a
raw score to a **z-score** and vice versa using formulas $z = (X - \bar{X})/s$ and $X = zs + \bar{X}$, respectively. Suppose that John, one of
the participants, had a self-persuasion score of 6. What
medical expert persuasion score should he have if he were
equally persuaded under both conditions? This problem requires
establishing John's **percentile rank** of his self-persuasion score
and then determining the medical expert persuasion score
(**percentile**) that has the same rank, or, alternatively,
comparing John's **standard scores** in both distributions.
Consider first the percentile rank of John's score, 6:

1. Although John's score, 6, is **discrete**, assume it has
   real limits and locate the interval containing the
   score. That interval is 5.5 – 6.5.
2. Determine the number of scores below John's score as
   follows:
   a. Count the number of scores falling below the assumed
      lower real limit (5.5). That number is 28.
   b. Compute the distance between the lower real limit
      and the specified score. That distance is 6 – 5.5 =
      0.5.
   c. Find out what proportion this distance is to the
      width (i) of the class. The proportion is 1/2 or
      0.5, that is 0.5/1 = 0.5.
   d. Determine the number of scores falling within this
      proportion of the class interval by multiplying the
      proportion by the frequency of the class interval as

follows: 0.5 x 7 = 3.5.

e. Calculate the number of scores falling below John's score by adding the number of scores (3.5) that are contained in the specified proportion of the interval to the number of scores (28) falling below the assumed lower real limit of the interval (5.5) as follows: 3.5 + 28 = 31.5.

3. Convert the total number of scores (31.5) falling below John's score to a percentile rank by putting it over the sum of the frequencies (50) and multiplying by 100 as follows: 31.5/50 x 100 = 63.

To maintain the same relative standing in the medical expert distribution that he has in the self-persuasion distribution, John's medical expert persuasion score would also have to have a **percentile rank** of 63. To find out what that score is, you must find the score value that is at the 63rd **percentile**, that is you must find P_{63}. This also can be accomplished by a step-by-step procedure.

1. Determine the number of scores that should fall below the specified percentile by taking k percent of the sum of the frequencies. In this example, the k in P_k = 63 and 0.63 x 50 = 31.5.

2. Locate the class interval containing P_k using the following procedure:

   a. Add up the scores in the frequency column beginning with the lowest class until you find adjacent cumulative frequencies that bracket the number of scores that fall below P_k. In this example those cumulative frequencies are 25 and 32.

   b. Select the class interval whose cumulative frequency is the highest of these two. That class is 10 − 11. The P_k is in this interval.

3. Determine P_k as follows:

   a. Determine the number of scores that fall between P_k and the lower real limit of the interval 10 − 11 by subtracting the number of scores (25) that fall below the lower real limit (9.5) of the class interval from the number of scores 31.5 that fall below P_k, 31.5 − 25 = 6.5.

   b. Convert this obtained value to a proportion by dividing it by the f of the interval 10 − 11. In this example, that proportion is 6.5/7 ≈ 0.93.

   c. Take this proportion (0.93) of the class interval width (i = 2), 0.93 x 2 = 1.86.

   d. Calculate the value for P_k by adding the 1.86 to the lower real limit 9.5, 1.86 + 9.5 = 11.36. Since the **dependent variable**, attitude change, is **operationally defined** as the number of attitudes or beliefs that change, the **dependent measure** is **discrete**. The 11.36, then, is rounded to the nearest whole number, that is 11.36 ≈ 11.

Eleven of John's attitudes or beliefs would have had to be

changed by the arguments of the medical experts for persuasion by the experts to be equal to John's self-persuasion.

Let's now see if John's self-persuasion **z-score** will lead to the same comparable medical expert persuasion **raw score**. The **mean** ($\bar{X}$) and **standard deviation** (**s**) of the self-persuasion distribution are 5.38 and 2.17, respectively. The **mean** ($\bar{X}$) and **standard deviation** (**s**) of the medical expert persuasion distribution are 9.82 and 4.96, respectively, (**you should verify these values**). John's self-persuasion **z-score** is, then, $z = (X - \bar{X})/s$ = (6 - 5.38)/2.17 $\approx$ 0.29. To find the **raw score** in the medical expert persuasion distribution you need to convert the **z-score** (0.29) to a **raw score** using the formula, $X = zs + \bar{X}$, as follows: X = 0.29(4.96) + 9.82 = 11.26 $\approx$ 11.

In this example the medical expert persuasion raw score needed to keep John at the same **relative standing** as his score in the self-persuasion distribution is 11 whether relative standing is determined by **percentile rank** or **a distance from the mean in standard deviation units**, that is, a **standard** or **z-score**.

Application Exercises

1. Assume Mary was also a participant in the studies described in the **Example Application**, and she has a self-persuasion score of 4.

   Determine

   a. the percentile rank of Mary's score.

   b. the score Mary would have to have to be at the 70th percentile.

   c. the quartile deviation of the self-persuasion distribution.

   d. the raw score in the medical experts' persuasion distribution that would have the same percentile rank as

Mary's score of 4 in the self-persuasion distribution.

e.   the z-score equivalent of Q_1 in the self-persuasion distribution.

f.   the standard score equivalent of Mary's self-persuasion score of 4.

g.   the score that Mary would have to have in the medical experts' persuasion distribution to maintain the same relative standing as her score of 4 in the self-persuasion distribution in terms of a distance from the mean in standard deviation units.

h.   the most appropriate graph(s) to make a comparison of Mary's relative standings in both distributions.

i.   the mode of the self-persuasion distribution.

j.   the median of the self-persuasion distribution.

2. Assume Henry was also a participant in the studies described in the **Example Application**, and he has a score in the medical experts' distribution of 15.

Determine

a. the percentile rank of Henry's score.

b. the score that Henry would have to have to be at the 90th percentile.

c. the semi-interquartile range of the medical experts' persuasion distribution.

d. the raw score in the self-persuasion that would have the same percentile rank as Henry's score of 15 in the medical experts' persuasion distribution.

e. the z-score equivalent of D_6 in the medical experts' persuasion distribution.

   f.   the standard score equivalent of Henry's score of 15.

   g.   the raw score in the self-persuasion distribution that would have the same z-score equivalent as Henry's score of 15 in the medical experts' persuasion distribution.

   h.   the most appropriate graph(s) to depict the data as presented in Table 7.1.

   i.   the mode of the medical experts' persuasion distribution.

   j.   the median of the medical experts' distribution.

MEETING THE CHALLENGE OF STATISTICS

The following problems pertain to the memory experiment described in the *Meeting the Challenge of Statistics* section in Chapter 1, pages 9-10, and the answers to that section in Chapter 3 of this workbook.

1. The simple frequency distribution in Table 7.2 is the answer to problem 3 of this section in Chapter 3.

Chapter 7

Table 7.2
Simple Frequency (*f*) Distribution of Recall Scores (*X*)
Presented in the *Meeting the Challenge of Statistics* Section
of Chapter 1 for the 60 Subjects

WORKSPACE FOR *s* AND $\overline{X}$ CALCULATIONS

X	f
18	2
17	0
16	5
15	5
14	4
13	9
12	7
11	9
10	5
9	7
8	4
7	0
6	2
5	1

Determine from Table 7.2

a. the quartile deviation.

b. the 35th percentile.

c. P_{15}.

    d.   the percentile rank of 14.

    e.   the standard score equivalent of 13.

    f.   the score that has a *z*-score equivalent of –1.0.

    g.   the score that is 2 standard deviations above the mean.

    h.   the raw score equivalent of *z* = +1.2.

2. In the space provided on the following page, construct a percent cumulative frequency curve for the percent cumulative frequency distribution in Table 7.3 which is the answer to problem 9 in this section of Chapter 3.

Table 7.3
Percent Cumulative Frequency Distribution of Recall Scores Presented in the *Meeting the Challenge of Statistics* Section of Chapter 1 with the Designated Criteria of $i = 2$ and $k = 7$

Class Interval	Frequency (*f*)	Cumulative Frequency	Percent Cumulative Frequency
17–18	2	60	100.0
15–16	10	58	96.7
13–14	13	48	80.0
11–12	16	35	58.3
9–10	12	19	31.7
7– 8	4	7	11.7
5– 6	3	3	5.0
	$\Sigma = 60$		

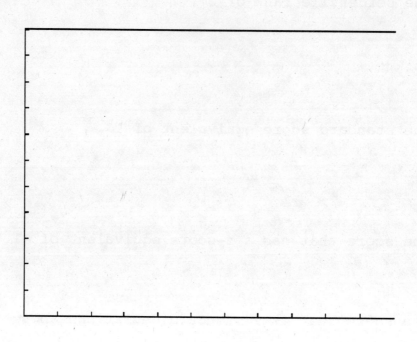

3. From the percent cumulative frequency curve in your answer to problem 2 estimate

   a. the percentile rank of 11.

   b. the 40th percentile.

   c. Q_3.

4. The grouped frequency distribution in Table 7.4, which has the same class intervals as Table 7.3, is the answer to problem 8 of this section in Chapter 3.

Table 7.4
Grouped Frequency Distribution of Recall Scores Presented in the *Meeting the Challenge of Statistics* Section in Chapter 1 with the Designated Criteria of $i = 2$ and $k = 7$

Class Interval Frequency (f)

Class Interval	Frequency (f)
17–18	2
15–16	10
13–14	13
11–12	16
9–10	12
7– 8	4
5– 6	3
	$\Sigma = 60$

Determine from Table 7.4

a. the percentile rank of 11.

b. the 40th percentile.

c. Q_3.

5. The grouped frequency distribution in Table 7.5 is the answer to problem 6 of this section in Chapter 3.

Table 7.5
Grouped Frequency Distribution of Recall Scores Presented in
the *Meeting the Challenge of Statistics* Section of Chapter 1
with the Designated Criteria of $i = 2$ and $k = 8$

Class Interval   Frequency (f)

Class Interval	Frequency (f)
18 – 19	2
16 – 17	5
14 – 15	9
12 – 13	16
10 – 11	14
8 – 9	11
6 – 7	2
4 – 5	1
	$\Sigma = 60$

From Table 7.5 determine

a. the z-score equivalent of 14.

b. the score that is 1.6 standard deviation units above the
    mean.

c. the score that has a standard score of –1.2.

d. the score that would have the same z-score equivalent of
    D_4 of the distribution in Table 7.4.

CHAPTER 8
MEASURES OF RELATIONSHIP

DETAILED TEXTBOOK OUTLINE

KEY TERMS AND DEFINITIONS

coefficient of determination Percentage or proportion of
    variance in one characteristic predictable from the other
    characteristic.

coefficient of nondetermination Percentage or proportion of variance in one characteristic that is not predictable from the other characteristic.

correlation The relationship between two variables or sample characteristics.

correlation coefficient An index of the degree of relationship between two variables or sample characteristics.

dichotomous A term referring to the fact that a variable can take on only one value or another.

least squares regression equation The regression equation that minimizes the square of the distances of the points from the line.

level of significance The probability level that is the dividing line between what is considered to be a high or low probability.

1 − r^2 Mathematical expression of the coefficient of nondetermination.

Pearson correlation coefficient or **r** An index of the relationship between two variables measured along interval or ratio scales.

phi coefficient or **r_ϕ** An index of the relationship between two dichotomous variables measured along nominal scales.

point-biserial coefficient or **r_{pb}** An index of the relationship between a variable measured along an interval or ratio scale and a dichotomous variable measured along a nominal scale.

r Symbol for the Pearson correlation coefficient.

regression The tendency for the predicted value of a variable to approach its mean value.

regression equation The equation for the best-fitting straight line through the points in a scatter plot.

regression line The line connecting the mean values of one characteristic for several fixed values of another characteristic.

$r = [N\Sigma XY-(\Sigma X)(\Sigma Y)]/\sqrt{[N\Sigma X^2-(\Sigma X)^2][N\Sigma Y^2-(\Sigma Y)^2]}$ Computational formula for the Pearson correlation coefficient.

ϱ (pronounced "rho") A symbol for the relationship between two population characteristics; the parameter equivalent of the statistic r.

r_{pb} Symbol for the point-biserial correlation coefficient.

r_ϕ Symbol for the phi-coefficient.

r_s Symbol for the Spearman rank-order correlation coefficient.

$r_s = 1 - 6\Sigma d^2/N(N^2 - 1)$ Computational formula for the Spearman correlation coefficient.

r^2 The coefficient of determination.

Spearman rank-order correlation coefficient or r_s An index of the relationship between two variables measured along ordinal scales.

standard error of prediction or $s_{Y'}$ The standard deviation of errors in prediction.

statistical hypothesis An assumption about a statistical population that one seeks to reject or fail to reject on the basis of information obtained from sample data.

statistical significance A condition in which the probability of occurrence is too low to warrant support of a statistical hypothesis.

$s_{Y'}$ Symbol for the standard error of prediction.

$s_{Y'} = s_Y \sqrt{1-r^2}$ Computational formula for obtaining the standard error of prediction.

$Y' = mX + b$ The regression equation.

MASTERING THE LANGUAGE OF STATISTICS

Fill-in-the-Blanks

Write the appropriate term(s) in the space(s) provided.

If each sample member is measured on two characteristics such as

weight and height, the relationship between the characteristics

is called the _____. An index or measure of the

degree of the relationship is called the _____

_____. One index, called the _____ correlation

coefficient, is a measure of the degree of relationship of two sample characteristics measured along interval or ratio scales. The letter _____ is used to symbolize the Pearson correlation coefficient. The parametric equivalent of r is _____, pronounced _____. Making an assumption about ϱ on the basis of r is called a statistical _____. In testing a statistical hypothesis about _____, you determine what the probability of obtaining your _____ would be if your hypothesis is correct. The hypothesis about ___ is generally that it equals zero. If the probability of obtaining your _____ when ϱ equals zero is too low, then you reject your _____

_____. The probability level that is the dividing line between what is considered a high or low probability is called the level of _____. Convention has been to set the level of _____ at 0.05 or 5%. The square of r is called the coefficient of _____. The coefficient of _____ is considered the proportion of variance in one characteristic predictable from the other characteristic. The coefficient of _____, then, is the proportion of variance in one characteristic that is not predictable from the other characteristic.

The Pearson correlation coefficient, _____, is used to indicate the degree of relationship between two characteristics when the measures of the characteristics constitute _____ or _____scales. When one characteristic is measured along an interval or ratio scale and the other is _____ —that is, can only be one thing or another—the _____ _____ correlation coefficient, symbolized _____, is used as an index

of the relationship. When both X and Y characteristics are

dichotomous, the _____ coefficient, _____, is used to index

the degree of the relationship. When the measures on both

characteristics constitute ordinal scales, the _____

_____ correlation coefficient, _____, is the

appropriate index. Although the formula for the Pearson

correlation coefficient can be used to obtain any of these

indices, there are more simplified formulas for ____, _____, and

_____. The simplified formula for r_s is _____ .

Even though a significant _____ does not imply a

cause and effect relationship, information about one

characteristic should provide information about the other. If

the relationship between two characteristics is a perfect

relationship, that is, if r = _____ or _____, the line

connecting the mean values of one characteristic at different

values of the other would be a straight line. The line

connecting the mean values for several fixed values of the other

characteristic is called the _____line. The equation

for the _____line is used to predict the value of one

characteristic for a known or given value of another

characteristic with which it is related. The term

_____ refers to the tendency for the predicted value

of one characteristic to more closely approach its mean value

for any given value of another characteristic. The equation for

the regression line is _____, where ____is the

predicted value, _____ is the slope of the line, and _____

is the point where the line crosses the Y-axis. The best-fitting straight line is one that gives the most satisfactory estimates of ____ and _____. The _____ _____ regression equation is believed to give the best estimates of m and b. Although the _____ _____ regression equation was developed to minimize errors in prediction, it does not necessarily eliminate errors. An error is the difference between the predicted value and the observed value of a characteristic. The standard deviation of these errors is called the _____ _____ of prediction.

True-False Items

Place a T for true and an F for False in the space provided before each item.

1. ____ The Pearson correlation coefficient is symbolized r_{pb}.

2. ____ The Pearson correlation coefficient is a measure of the degree of relationship of two sample characteristics measured along ordinal or interval scales.

3. ____ Correlation is depicted graphically by a scatter plot.

4. ____ Correlation refers to the relationship between two characteristics.

5. ____ An assumption about a statistical population is called a statistical hypothesis.

6. ____ A condition in which the probability of occurrence is too low to warrant support of a statistical hypothesis is called level of significance.

7. ____ The coefficient of nondetermination indicates the percentage of variability in one characteristic that is predictable from the other.

8. ____ When both X and Y characteristics are dichotomous and when the numbers assigned to the characteristics constitute nominal scales, the phi coefficient is used to index the degree of the relationship.

9. ____ The formula for r_{pb} is $1 - 6\Sigma d^2/N(N^2 - 1)$.

10._____ The line connecting mean values of one characteristic for several fixed values of another characteristic is called the regression line.

11._____ Regression refers to the tendency for the predicted value of one characteristic to more closely approach its maximum value than any other value.

12._____ The standard deviation of error scores is called the standard error of prediction.

Multiple-Choice Items

Blacken out the letter corresponding to the correct answer.

1. The percentage or proportion of variance in one characteristic predictable from the other is called
   (a) statistical significance.
   (b) coefficient of determination.
   (c) level of significance.
   (d) coefficient of nondetermination.

2. The mathematical expression of the coefficient of nondetermination is
   (a) $1 - r^2$.
   (b) r_{pb}.
   (c) r^2.
   (d) r_ϱ.

3. The symbol r_s represents the
   (a) Pearson correlation coefficient.
   (b) Spearman rank-order correlation coefficient.
   (c) phi coefficient.
   (d) point biserial correlation coefficient.

4. The symbol for the relationship between two population characteristics is
   (a) r_ϕ.
   (b) σ.
   (c) μ.
   (d) ϱ.

5. The correlation coefficient used with two dichotomous variables is
   (a) r.
   (b) r_{pb}.
   (c) r_ϕ.
   (d) r_s.

6. The probability level that is the dividing line between what is considered to be a high or low probability is called the
   (a) level of significance.

(b) coefficient of determination.
(c) probability constant.
(d) none of the above.

7. The correlation coefficient used when both variables are measured along an ordinal scale is
(a) r.
(b) r_s.
(c) r_{pb}.
(d) r_ϕ.

8. The tendency of the value of a characteristic to more closely approach its mean value than any other for a fixed value of another characteristic is called
(a) error in prediction.
(b) correlation.
(c) regression.
(d) least squares.

9. An index of the degree of relationship between two variables or sample characteristics is
(a) correlation.
(b) level of significance.
(c) regression.
(d) the correlation coefficient.

10. The relationship between two variables or sample characteristics is called
(a) correlation.
(b) level of significance.
(c) regression.
(d) the correlation coefficient.

11. The correlation coefficient used to index the relationship between two dependent variables measured along ratio scales is the
(a) Spearman rank-order coefficient.
(b) Pearson coefficient.
(c) point biserial coefficient.
(d) phi coefficient.

12. The formula $1 - 6\Sigma d^2/N(N^2 - 1)$ is used to compute
(a) r_{pb}.
(b) r.
(c) r_s.
(d) r_ϕ.

APPLYING STATISTICAL CONCEPTS

Example Application

Chapter 8

A question that continually resurfaces in the field of psychology is "which contributes more to human intelligence—heredity or environment?" One way this question is investigated is to measure the intelligence of identical twins reared apart. Identical twins have identical genetic makeup, whereas their environment, if they are reared apart, necessarily differs. A high **significant positive correlation** between the measures of intelligence of the identical twins reared apart is taken as evidence that heredity contributes more to human intelligence than environment.

A cognitive psychologist who believes that intelligence is to a large extent determined by heredity measures the intelligence of identical twins reared apart. Intelligence is **operationally defined** as the score achieved on an I.Q. test. The results obtained by the psychologist are shown in Table 8.1.

Table 8.1
The I.Q. Scores of Identical Twins Reared Apart. Twins Assigned Randomly As Twin 1 and Twin 2

| Twin Pair | Twin 1 | | Rank$_1$ | Twin 2 | | Rank$_2$ | | |
	X	X^2		Y	Y^2		XY	d^2
1	95	9025	1	100	10000	2	9500	1
2	100	10000	2	98	9604	1	9800	1
3	105	11025	3	106	11236	3	11130	0
4	108	11664	4	110	12100	5	11880	1
5	110	12100	5	112	12544	6	12320	1
6	112	12544	6	109	11881	4	12208	4
7	115	13225	7	117	13689	8	13455	1
8	120	14400	8	116	13456	7	13920	1
Σ	865	93983		868	94510		94213	10

Since I.Q. scores are generally considered to be along an interval scale, the **Pearson correlation coefficient** is used to index the degree of the relationship. The following is the formula for **r**, the **Pearson coefficient**:

$$r = \frac{N\Sigma XY - (\Sigma X)(\Sigma Y)}{\sqrt{[N\Sigma X^2 - (\Sigma X)^2][N\Sigma Y^2 - (\Sigma Y)^2]}}$$

Substituting the values from Table 8.1 for the appropriate symbols yields:

$$r = \frac{8(94213) - (865)(868)}{\sqrt{[8(93983) - (865)^2][8(94510) - (868)^2]}}$$

The value for *r* is approximately 0.93.

A value for r_s can also be obtained for the data in Table 8.1 by independently ranking the X and Y I.Q. scores as shown in Table 8.1. A difference score, d, is then obtained by subtracting the Y-ranks from the X-ranks. The sum of the squares of the d-scores are then substituted in the simplified formula for obtaining the **Spearman rank-order correlation coefficient** as follows:

$$r_s = 1 - \frac{6\Sigma d^2}{N(N^2-1)} = 1 - \frac{6(10)}{8(64-1)} = 0.88$$

Comparing the obtained value (0.93) of *Pearson correlation coefficient*, r, with the table value (0.71) of r in textbook appendix Table 2 that is associated with a 5 percent **significance level** for a sample with $N - 2$ **degrees of freedom**, you would reject the **statistical hypothesis** that $\varrho = 0$ and conclude that the obtained r-value indicates a significant relationship between the I.Q scores of identical twins reared apart. Squaring r gives you the **coefficient of determination** (r^2) which tells you the percentage or proportion of variability in Y I.Q. scores that is predictable from the variability in the X I.Q. scores which in this case is 86.49%. Subtracting r^2 from 1 gives you the **coefficient of nondetermination**, the percentage of variability in the Y-scores that cannot be from the variability in the X-scores, which in this case is 13.5%.

Once a *significant correlation* has been obtained, a straight line, called the **regression line**, can be fitted to the points in the **scatter plot** that depicts the relationship between the I.Q. scores. This is accomplished by calculating the **least squares regression equation**. The equation for the straight line allows you to predict values for Y-scores given specific values for X. The **regression equation** is $Y' = mX + b$, where m indicates the slope of the line and b is the Y-intercept. The value for m is obtained by solving the following two equations simultaneously:

$$N\Sigma XY = Nm\Sigma X^2 + Nb\Sigma X$$
$$\Sigma X\Sigma Y = m(\Sigma X)^2 + Nb\Sigma X$$

[1] $8(94213) = 8m(93983) + 8b(865)$
[2] $(865)(868) = m(865)^2 + 8b(865)$

Subtracting the bottom equation [2] from the top equation [1] and dividing both sides of the resulting equation by the coefficient of m (3639) gives the value 0.79 for m. Substituting this value for m in the top equation [1] and solving for b yields the value 23.08. The regression equation then is:

$$Y' = 0.79X + 23.08$$

Substituting any value for X (Twin 1's I.Q.) will yield the predicted value of Y (Twin 2's I,Q.). For example, if Twin 1's I.Q. is 109, the predicted value for Twin 2's I.Q is 109.

$$Y' = 0.79(109) + 23.08 = 109$$

114

Chapter 8

Application Exercises

1. Another way psychologists have attempted to examine the heredity-environment question posed in the *Example Application* is to determine the relationship between a child's I.Q and a biological parent's I.Q. The following pairs of numbers (*X*, *Y*) are the I.Q. scores of biological parent and child, respectively: (120, 123), (101, 100), (119, 117), (125, 127), (98, 103), (102, 110), (105, 100), (113, 107), (123, 131), (120, 118).

   Determine

   a. an arrangement of parents' scores in ascending order.

   b. an arrangement of childrens' scores in ascending order.

   c. the scale of measurement.

   d. the range of the parents' scores.

   e. an arrangement of the data as set up in Table 8.1 of the Example Application where parents' scores are the *X*-values.

   _____
   _____
   _____
   _____
   _____
   _____
   _____
   _____
   _____
   _____
   _____
   _____
   _____
   _____
   _____

   f. the three measures of central tendency for the parents' scores.

g. the three measures of central tendency for the children's scores.

h. the variance and standard deviation of the parents' scores.

i. the variance and standard deviation of the children's scores.

j. the I.Q score a child should have to be the same distance from the mean in standard deviation units as a parent with an I.Q. score of 105.

k. the value for the Pearson correlation coefficient.

l. the value of the Spearman rank-order correlation coefficient.

    m. if r and r_s are significant at the 5% level of significance.

    n. the coefficients of determination and nondetermination.

    o. the regression equation.

    p. the predicted value of a child's I.Q who has a parent with an I.Q. of 115.

    q. the standard error of prediction.

2. The psychologist who collected the biological parent-child I.Q. data in problem 1 of this section also collected I.Q. data on foster parents and foster children to examine further the heredity-environment question posed in the *Example Application*.

    The following pairs of numbers (X,Y) are the I.Q. scores of foster parent and child, respectively: (120, 115), (112, 107), (125, 107), (109, 112), (100, 115), (105, 112), (128, 128), (105,120), (113, 120), (105, 100).

Determine

   a. an arrangement of parents' scores in ascending order.

   b. an arrangement of childrens' scores in ascending order.

   c. an arrangement of the data as set up in Table 8.1 of the Example Application where parents' scores are the *X*-values.

   _____
   _____
   _____
   _____
   _____
   _____
   _____
   _____
   _____
   _____
   _____
   _____
   _____
   _____

   d. the three measures of central tendency for the parents' scores.

   e. the three measures of central tendency for the childrens' scores.

   f. the variance and standard deviation of the parents' scores.

g.   the variance and standard deviation of the children's scores.

h.   the child's score that has a z-score equivalent of 1.8.

i.   the parent's score that has the same z-score equivalent of a child's score of 110.

j.   the value for the Pearson correlation coefficient.

k.   the percentage of variability in the children's scores that can be predicted from the variability in the parents' scores.

l.   the statistical hypothesis being tested.

m.   if r is significant at the 5% level of significance.

   n.   a conclusion about the statistical hypothesis.

   o. r_s.

   p.   if r_s is significant at the 0.05 level of significance.

MEETING THE CHALLENGE OF STATISTICS

The following problems pertain to the memory experiment described in the *Meeting the Challenge of Statistics* section in Chapter 1, pages 9-10, of this workbook. The data set for the experimental group presented emotion laden words follow and are to be used to answer the problems in this section.

Emotion Laden Words (pleasant, **unpleasant**) Experimental: (9,6), (10,8), (9,7), (8,8), (7,6), (9,7), (10,6), (8,5), (7,8), (9,9)

For this data set

1. Construct a scatter plot with the number of pleasant words recalled along the *X*-axis in the space provided.

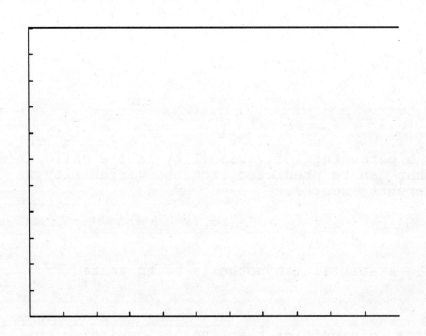

2. Organize the data in a Table Format similar to that of Table 8.1.

_____
_____
_____
_____
_____
_____
_____
_____
_____
_____
_____
_____
_____
_____

3. Compute the value for the Pearson correlation coefficient.

4. State the statistical hypothesis being tested.

5. Calculate the degrees of freedom.

6. Determine if the calculated r is significant at the 5% level of significance.

7. Reach a conclusion about the statistical hypothesis.

8. If appropriate, determine the regression equation; if not appropriate, tell why.

9. Rank independently the pleasant and unpleasant words correctly recalled in your table in problem 2 of this section and compute the Spearman rank order correlation coefficient.

10. Determine if r_s is significant at the 5% level of significance.

CHAPTER 9
PROBABILITY AND DECISION MAKING

DETAILED TEXTBOOK OUTLINE

Review Exercises (Page 204)

Answers to Progress Assessments (Page 206)

KEY TERMS AND DEFINITIONS

α (pronounced "alpha") The symbol used to represent alpha level, that is, the probability of making an alpha error.

alpha error or **Type I error** An error an investigator makes when a true null hypothesis is rejected.

alpha level or **level of significance** The probability level used in a decision rule.

alternative hypothesis or H_1 A mathematical statement about a population characteristic based on what an investigator believes to be true as described in the investigator's research hypothesis.

β (pronounced "beta") The symbol used to represent the probability of making a Type II error.

beta error or **Type II error** An error an investigator makes when a false hypothesis is not rejected.

classical view of probability A definition of probability based on logical analyses and mathematical models where probability is defined as a ratio based on the number of times a given event can occur divided by the total number of all possible events that are equally likely to occur.

decision rule The specific values of a test statistic that are necessary to reject or not reject a null hypothesis for a given level of significance.

empirical frequency distributions Frequency distributions based on collected data.

empirical view of probability A definition of probability based on a large number of previous observations indicating whether or not the event has occurred. Probability is given as a ratio based on the number of times an event has occurred divided by the number of observations.

H_0 The symbol used to represent the null hypothesis.

H_1 The symbol used to represent the alternative hypothesis.

normal curve The graphic representation of the normal distribution.

Chapter 9

normal distribution A specific theoretical frequency distribution of a continuous variable based on an infinite number of scores which is characterized by its bell shape and symmetry. It is used frequently by investigators to estimate the probability of occurrence of empirical events.

normal distribution table or **normal curve table** A listing of the relationship between z-scores and percent area of the normal curve based on the normal distribution.

null hypothesis or H_0 A mathematical statement about a population characteristic based on what an investigator believes to be false as described in the investigator's research hypothesis. It is the negation of the alternative hypothesis.

$p(A) = n_A/n_{total}$ A computational formula for determining the probability of an event (A).

power The probability of correctly rejecting a false null hypothesis.

probability A percentage or proportion indicating the likelihood of occurrence of some specified event (or events).

research hypothesis A statement describing the relationship between certain events, that can be tested empirically. An experimental research hypothesis describes how changes in an independent variable cause changes in a dependent variable. A correlational research hypothesis states whether events are or are not related to each other in a systematic fashion.

subjective view of probability A definition of probability based on a measure of the strength of one's belief that an event will or will not occur.

statistical hypothesis A mathematical statement about one or more characteristics of a given population.

statistical test A set of procedures used to evaluate a statistical hypothesis.

test statistics Statistics that are used to determine the probability of certain events described in relation to a null hypothesis as happening on the basis of chance.

theoretical frequency distribution A hypothetical frequency distribution based on logical analyses and mathematical models.

Chapter 9

MASTERING THE LANGUAGE OF STATISTICS

Fill-in-the-Blanks

Write the appropriate term(s) in the space(s) provided.

To statistically analyze data in a way that they can be related
to a particular _____ hypothesis requires a thorough
understanding of _____, a proportion or percentage
indicating the likelihood of occurrence of some specified event
(or events). There are three views of _____: (1) the
_____ view, according to which _____ is a measure
of the strength of one's belief that an event will or will not
occur; (2) the _____view, according to which _____
is the ratio of the number of times an event occurred divided by
the number of observations; and (3) the _____ view, which
defines _____ as the ratio of the number of times a
specified event can occur to the number of all possible events
that are equally likely to occur. According to this latter
view, the _____ of the event A can be determined by the
following formula: $p(A) = $ _____.

   In the empirical sciences, probability is generally
calculated on the basis of _____ frequency
distributions which are based on logical analyses and
mathematical models instead of on the basis of _____
frequency distributions which are based on collected data. A(n)
_____ frequency distribution that is extremely useful in
empirical research is the _____ distribution. The
graphic representation of the _____ distribution is called

126

the _____ curve which is characterized by its bell shape
and symmetry. When using the _____ curve to determine the
probability of specified events, the _____ _____
table is most often used. The _____ _____ table is a
listing of the relationship between z-scores and percent area of
the _____ _____. The z-scores are called _____
_____ and are used to make decisions about the truthfulness
of certain _____ hypotheses, which are statements about
one or more characteristics of a given population. The
_____ hypothesis generally evaluated is called the
_____ hypothesis and is symbolized, H_0. The _____
_____ is the negation of the _____ hypothesis,
symbolized _____.   The _____ hypothesis is the
translation of the _____ hypothesis into a mathematical
statement.

The set of procedures used to evaluate the null hypothesis
is called a statistical _____. Applying a statistical test
requires that a _____ rule be formed and a _____
_____ calculated. On the basis of your statistical _____
you make a decision to reject or fail to reject the
_____ hypothesis. If you reject the _____ hypothesis you
accept the _____ hypothesis. Accepting the _____
hypothesis lends support to the _____ hypothesis.

When using a statistical _____ to make decisions about the
_____ hypothesis, errors can be made. Rejecting a true
hypothesis is an error called the _____ or _____error.
The probability of making this error is symbolized _____.

Chapter 9

Failing to reject a false null hypothesis leads to an error called the _____ or _____ error. The probability of making this error is symbolized _____. The probability of correctly rejecting a false hypothesis is called the _____ of the test and is symbolized _____.

True-False Items

Place a T for true or an F for false in the space provided before each item.

1. ____ According to the empirical view of probability, probability is based on one's belief that an event will or will not happen.

2. ____ The ratio of the number of times an event occurred to the number of observations is the classical view of probability.

3. ____ The empirical view of probability requires that the number of observations be large enough for probability to be measured.

4. ____ The formula $p(A) = n_A/n_{total}$ represents the classical view of probability.

5. ____ Distributions based on collected data are called theoretical frequency distributions.

6. ____ Frequency distributions based on logical analyses and mathematical models, not on actual collected data, are called normal distributions.

7. ____ The normal distribution is bell-shaped and symmetrical.

8. ____ For the normal curve there is a constant relationship between the area under the curve and the distance along the X-axis.

9. ____ A statement describing the relationship between certain events that can be empirically tested is called a statistical hypothesis.

10. ____ The null hypothesis, symbolized H_1, is formed by negating the alternative hypothesis.

11. ____ The beta error refers to rejecting a true hypothesis.

Chapter 9

12.____ The power of a test refers to the probability of rejecting a false hypothesis.

Multiple-Choice Items

Blacken out the letter corresponding to the correct answer.

1. The view of probability that defines probability on the basis of a ratio where the number of times a given event can occur is divided by the total number of all possible events is the
   - (a) empirical view.
   - (b) classical view.
   - (c) subjective view.
   - (d) normal view.

2. Frequency distributions based on actual collected data are called
   - (a) normal distributions.
   - (b) theoretical distributions.
   - (c) empirical distributions.
   - (d) statistical distributions.

3. A statement describing the relationship between certain events that can be empirically tested is called
   - (a) a research hypothesis.
   - (b) a statistical hypothesis.
   - (c) the null hypothesis.
   - (d) the alternative hypothesis.

4. The research hypothesis as the investigator believes it to be true is translated into a mathematical statement called
   - (a) a formula.
   - (b) a test statistic.
   - (c) the null hypothesis.
   - (d) none of the above.

5. A set of procedures used to evaluate a statistical hypothesis is called
   - (a) a statistical test.
   - (b) a test statistic.
   - (c) a decision rule.
   - (d) level of significance.

6. The decision rule most frequently used in the behavioral sciences is that H_0 should be rejected if the probability of obtaining the calculated test statistic is
   - (a) ≥ 0.05.
   - (b) ≤ 0.05.
   - (c) ≥ 0.01.
   - (d) ≤ 0.01.

7. Failing to reject a false hypothesis is
   (a) not an error.
   (b) a beta error.
   (c) an alpha error.
   (d) a Type III error.

8. The probability of correctly rejecting a false hypothesis is
   (a) α.
   (b) $1 - \alpha$.
   (c) β.
   (d) $1 - \beta$.

9. A Type II error is
   (a) a beta error.
   (b) the error of rejecting a true H_0.
   (c) an alpha error.
   (d) both *b* and *c*.

10. The probability level used in a decision rule is
    (a) α.
    (b) β.
    (c) $1 - \alpha$.
    (d) $1 - \beta$.

11. The area of the normal curve that falls between μ and $z = -1.0$ is
    (a) the same as the area that falls between μ and $z = +1.0$.
    (b) 0.3413 proportion of the total area under the curve.
    (c) 34.13% of the total area of the curve.
    (d) all of the above.

12. The probability of incorrectly rejecting a true null hypothesis is
    (a) the level of significance.
    (b) the power of the test.
    (c) beta.
    (d) $1 - \alpha$.

APPLYING STATISTICAL CONCEPTS

Example Application

Cognitive psychologists are interested in how we form concepts, that is, the rules we use to classify things as belonging to a particular group or category. A distinction is made between types of concepts. A conjunctive concept is defined by the presence of a set of attributes. For example, father is a conjunctive concept. A father must be male *and* have a child. A disjunctive concept is defined by any one of a set of characteristics. Children is a disjunctive concept. Children can be girls *or* boys. A cognitive psychologist believes that

instructions play a role in concept formation in a laboratory
setting. A limited pool of subjects is randomly divided into
two groups. Each group is given a concept formation test in
which ten different disjunctive concepts must be formed. One
group is instructed that they are to form disjunctive concepts;
the other group is not given that instruction. The amount of
time each subject takes to form the 10 concepts constitutes the
data collected. The psychologist computes and compares the mean
times of the two groups. He finds that the observed difference
between the means would occur only 3% of the time if the
instructions had no effect.

If you can apply to this hypothetical study what is said
about evaluating hypotheses in Chapter 9 of the textbook, you
can make the following statements. The **research hypothesis** is
that instructions will influence concept formation. This
hypothesis can be translated into a **statistical hypothesis**.
This statistical hypothesis is called the **alternative hypothesis**
and is symbolized H_1: $\mu_{instruction} \neq \mu_{no\ instruction}$. Negating the
alternative hypothesis gives the **null hypothesis**, H_0: $\mu_{instruction} =
\mu_{no\ instruction}$. The **decision rule** is reject H_0 if $p \leq 0.05$. Since
the probability of occurrence of the obtained difference in
means based on a **theoretical frequency distribution** is only 3%
and the **significance level** is 0.05, H_0 is rejected. The
statistical evidence is taken by the psychologist to support the
research hypothesis. The psychologist, however, could possibly
be making an **alpha** or **Type I error**. The probability of making
such an error in this case is $\alpha = 0.05$, the **level of
significance**.

Assume that for 10,000 people taking the concept formation
test without instructions, as in our hypothetical study, the
distribution of times to form the ten concepts approximates the
normal distribution with a mean equal to 96 minutes and a
standard deviation equal to 8 minutes. Applying what you have
learned about the normal distribution, the normal curve, and the
normal curve table, you should be able to determine the number
of people who formed the ten concepts in less than 80 minutes.
You first draw a diagram indicating the area of the **normal curve**
that represents a solution to the problem (see Figure 9.1). You
then convert 80 minutes to a **standard** or **z-score** as follows: $z =
(X - \mu)/\sigma = (80 - 96)/8 = -2$. Mark this value on your diagram.
Use the **normal distribution table**, Appendix Table 4, to fill in
the appropriate areas on your diagram expressed as proportions
as shown in Figure 9.1. Determine the answer by examining the
diagram and performing the appropriate arithmetic calculations.
Examining the curve you see that the proportion beyond $z = -2$ is
0.0228. Taking this proportion of 10,000, then, yields a value,
228, the number of people who formed the 10 concepts in less
than 80 minutes.

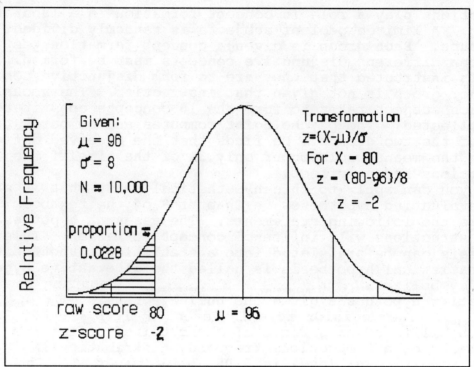

Figure 9.1. Drawing used to illustrate procedure for solving normal curve problems.

Application Exercises

1. Our perception of visual stimuli can vary as a function of factors such as attention, motivation, past experience, social environment, and so forth. A social psychologist believes that perception of the size of coins will differ as a function of economic status. Children from two distinct economic backgrounds (family income under $15,000 and family income over $40,000) are randomly selected to participate in the study. Each child is asked to draw the size of each of a United States cent, nickel, dime, quarter and half dollar. The difference between the drawn size and the actual size of the coins is computed and averaged for each child. A mean group score is then computed and compared. The psychologist determines that the probability of obtaining the observed difference in means if there were no effect of economic status on perception of coin size is 0.04.

    Specify

    a. the research hypothesis based on the psychologist's belief about the event of interest.

   b. the mathematical statement (alternative hypothesis) of
       the research hypothesis.

   c. the negation of the alternative hypothesis (null
       hypothesis).

   d. a decision rule.

   e. the decision made concerning the null hypothesis based
       on the decision rule and the probability of obtaining
       these results if economic status did not affect
       perception of coin size in children.

   f. what the decision about the null hypothesis means in
       terms of the research hypothesis.

   g. the type of error that can be made based on the decision
       about the null hypothesis.

2. How one measures fear in animals has always been of concern
   to animal behaviorists. One measure that is frequently used
   with laboratory rodents is based on the observation that
   frightened rodents tend to become immobile. When such an
   immobility response is conditioned it is called a
   conditioned emotional response. An emotional response can
   easily be conditioned by pairing an innocuous stimulus such
   as a light with a fear provoking stimulus such as a loud
   noise. When the light takes on fear evoking properties, the
   emotional response is said to be conditioned. How fear
   evoking the light becomes as a result of the conditioning is
   determined by how long the animal remains immobile when the
   light is presented. An animal behaviorist interested in how
   the measure of fear is distributed in a population of 2000
   rats records the length of time each of the 2000 rats
   remains immobile after being presented a light to which an
   emotional response has been conditioned. Table 9.1 presents
   the results.

Table 9.1
A frequency distribution of the time in seconds rats remain immobile after being presented a light to which an emotional response has been conditioned (N = 2000)

Class Interval (Time in seconds)	f	
160 – 169	7	
150 – 159	12	
140 – 149	13	
130 – 139	73	
120 – 129	103	
110 – 119	163	
100 – 109	213	
90 – 99	274	
80 – 89	284	
70 – 79	274	
60 – 69	213	
50 – 59	163	
40 – 49	103	
30 – 39	73	
20 – 29	13	
10 – 19	12	
00 – 09	7	

For the data in Table 9.1, determine

a. the mean (μ) using the method of transformed scores.

b. the median and the mode.

c. the shape of the distribution based on your answers to parts *a* and *b*.

d. the standard deviation (σ) of the population of rats using the method of transformed scores. Note, in computing sigma, the sum of the squared deviations from the mean is divided by the population size (2000).

e. Q_1 using the procedure described in Chapter 7 of the textbook.

f. the percentile rank of 80 using the procedure described in Chapter 7 of the textbook.

g. the number of rats remaining immobile for at least 60 seconds using μ and σ computed in parts *a* and *d*, and the normal curve table (Appendix Table 4).

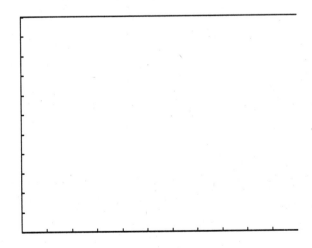

h. the probability of randomly selecting a rat who remains immobile more than 2 minutes when the light is presented (Use μ, σ, and the normal curve table).

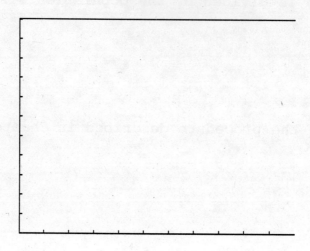

i. the percentile rank of 80 using μ, σ, and the normal curve table.

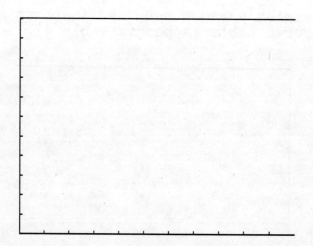

j. Q_1 using the normal curve table.

k. the percentage of rats that have immobility scores between 120 and 150 seconds using the normal curve table.

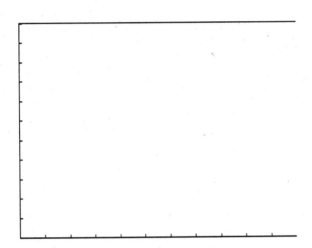

MEETING THE CHALLENGE OF STATISTICS

The following problems pertain to the memory experiment described in the *Meeting the Challenge of Statistics* section in Chapter 1, pages 9-10, of this workbook.

1. State the research hypothesis based on the student's interest in the effect of sleep on the recall of verbal material.

2. Form the alternative statistical hypothesis by translating the research hypothesis into a mathematical statement about the means of the populations from which the experimental and control groups were selected.

3. Negate the alternative statistical hypothesis (H_1) and state this negation as the null hypothesis (H_0).

4. Formulate a decision rule that would allow you to reject H_0 at a given alpha level. Use the alpha level most often used in the behavioral sciences.

5. Assume that the probability of obtaining the observed difference in the means of the experimental and control groups is *less* than 5% if there were no effects of sleep on recall of verbal material. What decision would you make about the null hypothesis?

6. What does your decision mean in terms of the research hypothesis?

7. What kind of error could you possibly make?

8. Assume that the probability of obtaining the observed difference in the means of the experimental and control groups is *greater* than 5% if there were no effects of sleep on the recall of verbal material. What decision would you make about the null hypothesis?

9. What does your decision in part *8* mean in terms of the research hypothesis?

10. What error could your decision in part *9* lead to?

CHAPTER 10
SAMPLING DISTRIBUTIONS, INFERENTIAL STATISTICS, AND HYPOTHESIS EVALUATION

DETAILED TEXTBOOK OUTLINE

KEY TERMS AND DEFINITIONS

central limit theorem A mathematical theorem that describes the sampling distribution of sample means. According to this theorem, if sample size is large ($N \geq 30$), the sampling distribution of the mean approaches a normal distribution with $\mu_{\bar{x}}$ and $\sigma_{\bar{x}} = \sigma/\sqrt{N}$.

critical regions Areas of a sampling distribution that include values which are not likely to be due to chance.

critical values Specific values that mark off the critical regions of a sampling distribution.

expected value The mean of a sampling distribution.

general decision rule A rule that specifies the conditions under which H_0 is rejected.

k The symbol used to represent the number of samples.

$\mu_{\bar{x}}$ The symbol used to represent the expected value of the sampling distribution of the mean.

$\mu_{\bar{x}} = \mu$ An equality stated in the central limit theorem used to determine the expected value of a sampling distribution of the mean when μ is known.

nondirectional statistical hypotheses Statistical hypotheses used when the investigator has no reason to predict that the statistic will be either above or below the parameter given in the null hypothesis.

p The symbol used to indicate the probability of obtaining a calculated statistic on the basis of chance.

sampling distribution A theoretical distribution of a particular statistic for an infinite number of random samples of a given size from a population of an infinite size.

sampling distribution of the mean, $\bar{X}$ A theoretical distribution of an infinite number of means from random samples of a specified size.

$\sigma_{\bar{x}}$ The symbol used to represent the standard error of the sampling distribution of the mean.

$\sigma_{\bar{x}} = \sqrt{\dfrac{\Sigma(\bar{X})^2 - (\Sigma\bar{X})^2/k}{k}}$ A formula used to calculate the standard error of a sampling distribution of the mean.

$\sigma_{\bar{x}} = \sigma/\sqrt{N}$ An equality stated in the central limit theorem used to calculate the standard error of a sampling distribution of the mean when σ and sample size are known.

$\Sigma(\bar{X} - \mu_{\bar{x}}) = 0$ The defining equation of the expected value of the sampling distribution of the mean.

specific decision rule A statement involving values of an identified test statistic that indicates when H_0 is to be rejected at a given alpha level.

specific decision rule for z when alpha equals 0.05 If $|z_{calc}| \geq$ 1.96, reject the null hypothesis.

standard error The standard deviation of a sampling distribution.

two-tailed statistical test A statistical test that requires that H_0 be rejected if the test statistic is located at either extreme end of the theoretical sampling distribution.

z = $(\bar{X} - \mu_{\bar{x}})/\sigma_{\bar{x}}$ The formula for the z-statistic used when working with a sampling distribution of the mean.

MASTERING THE LANGUAGE OF STATISTICS

Fill-in-the-Blanks

Theoretical distributions, called _____ distributions, are used by investigators to test hypotheses about population parameters. A _____ _____ is a theoretical distribution of a particular statistic for an infinite number of random samples of a specified size. The _____ _____ of the _____, then, is a theoretical distribution of an infinite number of means. The mean of a sampling distribution is called its _____ _____. The standard deviation of a sampling distribution is called the _____ _____.

Chapter 10

The symbol _____ represents the expected value of the sampling distribution of the mean. The defining equation for the expected value is _____. The standard error of the sampling distribution of the mean is symbolized _____. The formula used to calculate the standard error of the sampling distribution of the mean is _____.

According to the _____ _____ theorem, as the sample size increases, the sampling distribution of the mean approaches the shape of the normal distribution regardless of shape of the distribution of the population from which the samples are selected. For very large samples _____ equals μ. The sampling distribution of the mean has a _____ _____, symbolized _____, equal to the standard deviation of the population from which the samples are selected divided by the square root of the sample size. This equality is symbolized _____.

The sampling distribution of the mean is often used to test hypotheses called _____ _____ hypotheses, which are used when the investigator has no reason to predict that the statistic will be either above or below the parameter stated in the null hypothesis. A _____-_____ _____ test is used to evaluate a nondirectional statistical hypotheses. Regions of the sampling distribution of the mean that include values of a test statistic that are not likely to be due to chance are called _____ _____. The specific values that mark off the critical regions are called _____ _____. These values are used in conjunction with a _____ decision rule which, like a _____ decision rule, specifies

the conditions under which H_0 is rejected. A general decision

rule specifies the probability (symbolized ____) of obtaining a

calculated test statistic on the basis of chance. A _____

decision rule specifies the values of test statistics that will

lead to a rejection of H_0. The specific decision rule for z

when alpha is equal to 0.05 is

_____.

True-False Items

*Place a T for true or an F for false in the space provided
before each item.*

1.____ The mean of a sampling distribution is called its
expected value.

2.____ The mean of a sampling distribution is symbolized $\bar{X}$.

3.____ The variability in a sampling distribution is called its
standard error.

4.____ The standard error of the sampling distribution of the
mean is symbolized $\sigma_{\bar{x}}$.

5.____ According to the central limit theorem, as the sample
size decreases, the sampling distribution of the mean
approaches a normal distribution.

6.____ Hypotheses used when an investigator has no reason to
predict that the test statistic will be either above or
below the parameter stated in the null hypothesis are
called nondirectional hypotheses.

7.____ Those areas of a distribution that include values of the
test statistic that are not likely to occur on the basis
of chance are called critical regions.

8.____ The values that mark off critical regions are called
specific values.

9.____ A specific decision rule specifies the probability at
which H_0 is rejected.

10.____ $\sigma_{\bar{x}} = \sigma/\sqrt{N}$.

Chapter 10

11. _____ $\mu_{\bar{x}} = \mu$.

12. _____ When working with a sampling distribution of the mean based on a large N, the z-formula is $z = (\bar{X} - \mu_{\bar{x}})/\sigma_{\bar{x}}$.

Multiple-Choice Items

Blacken out the letter corresponding to the correct answer.

1. The mean of a sampling distribution is called
   (a) $\bar{X}$.
   (b) the average.
   (c) the expected value.
   (d) the standard error.

2. The defining equation for the sampling distribution of the mean is
   (a) $z = (\bar{X} - \mu_{\bar{x}})/\sigma_{\bar{x}}$.
   (b) $\Sigma(X - \bar{X}) = 0$.
   (c) $z = (X - \bar{X})/s$.
   (d) $\Sigma(\bar{X} - \mu_{\bar{x}}) = 0$.

3. $\sigma_{\bar{x}}$ equals
   (a) $\sigma/\sqrt{N}$.
   (b) the standard error of the mean.
   (c) the standard deviation of the sampling distribution of the mean.
   (d) all of the above.

4. The correct order of steps in hypothesis evaluation is
   (a) form a research hypothesis, form a testable statistical hypothesis, and perform a statistical test.
   (b) form a testable statistical hypothesis, perform a statistical test, and form a research hypothesis.
   (c) form a research hypothesis, perform a statistical test, and form a statistical hypothesis.
   (d) perform a statistical test, form a statistical hypothesis, and form a research hypothesis.

5. Which of the following is most likely to be a nondirectional statistical hypothesis?
   (a) $\mu_{\bar{x}} \leq 20$
   (b) $\mu_{\bar{x}} > 20$
   (c) $\mu_{\bar{x}} < 20$
   (d) $\mu_{\bar{x}} = 20$

6. Which of the following is a general decision rule?
   (a) if $|z_{calc}| \geq 1.96$, reject H_0
   (b) reject H_0 if $p(\bar{X} = 20) = 0.05$
   (c) $H_0: \mu_{\bar{x}} = 20$
   (d) none of the above

7. The symbol used to indicate the probability of obtaining a calculated statistic on the basis of chance is
   (a) k.
   (b) p.
   (c) μ.
   (d) N.

8. For the normal distribution critical values are usually expressed as
   (a) z-scores.
   (b) means.
   (c) two-tailed statistics.
   (d) none of the above.

9. Values that mark off critical regions are called
   (a) regional values.
   (b) z-scores.
   (c) critical values.
   (d) two-tailed statistics.

10. When reporting the outcome of a statistical test you are required to
    (a) name the test statistic.
    (b) specify the population size.
    (c) use a nondirectional statistical hypothesis.
    (d) do all of the above.

11. A two-tailed statistical test requires that H_0 be rejected if
    (a) the calculated statistic can be plus or minus.
    (b) the calculated statistic is at the upper tail of the distribution.
    (c) the calculated statistic has two tails.
    (d) the calculated statistic is located at either extreme end of the sampling distribution.

12. When reporting the outcome of a statistical test you are required to
    (a) describe what the outcome means with respect to the research hypothesis.
    (b) name the test statistic.
    (c) specify the degrees of freedom or, in some cases, the sample size.
    (d) do all of the above.

APPLYING STATISTICAL CONCEPTS

Example Application

Assume that in the world population the intelligence of children defined in terms of the score—intelligence quotient (IQ)—on a standardized intelligence test is normally distributed. The standard deviation of this distribution is 15, which means that approximately 68 percent of the population of children will have an IQ score between 85 and 115. Assume further that a sample of 36 children selected from this population has a mean ($\bar{X}$) equal to 105. Is it likely that this sample represents a random sample from the population?

If you understood the material in chapter 10 of the textbook you would know that to answer the question posed you must consider a **sampling distribution** based on a sample of size N = 36. The specific **sampling distribution** is the **sampling distribution of the mean**. This **sampling distribution** has an **expected value**, $\mu_{\bar{x}}$, equal to 100, the mean (μ) of the population, and a **standard error**, $\sigma_{\bar{x}}$, equal to $\sigma/\sqrt{N}$, that is 15/6 = 2.5. To answer the question posed you should follow the steps listed in the section *Putting It All Together* in Chapter 10 of the textbook.

1. *State the research hypothesis.* If you wish to determine if the selected sample comes from a population with μ = 100 and σ = 15, you must have some reason to suspect that it does not. Your research hypothesis, therefore, is that the sample does not represent a random sample from the specified population.

2. *Translate the research hypothesis into a set of mutually exclusive and exhaustive mathematically statements* by (a) forming an alternative hypothesis (H_1) that is in agreement with the research hypothesis and by (b) negating H_1 to form the null hypothesis (H_0). In the example:

$$H_0: \mu_{\bar{x}} = 100$$
$$H_1: \mu_{\bar{x}} \neq 100$$

3. *Perform a statistical test* in the following manner:
   a. Identify a test statistic. In the example the test statistic is **z** since the sample size is relatively large and the theoretical distribution of interest is the sampling distribution of the mean, which approaches the normal distribution.
   b. Select alpha. For this example, as is usually the case, set α = 0.05.
   c. Form a decision rule. For this example, since α = 0.05, the decision rule is if $|z_{calc}| \geq 1.96$, reject H_0.
   d. Calculate the test statistic. For the example, z = ($\bar{X} - \mu_{\bar{x}})/\sigma_{\bar{x}}$ = (105 – 100)/2.5 = 2.
   e. Determine the probability of obtaining a sample mean that would deviate from the mean of the sampling distribution by as much as 2. Using the normal distribution table, the probability is 0.0456.

4. *Reach a decision about H_0.* For the example, since 2 is greater than 1.96, reject H_0.

5. *Make a decision about the research hypothesis.* In the example, the belief that the sample does not represent a random sample is supported.

6. *Report the results of your statistical test.* This requires
   a. describing what the outcome means with respect to the research hypothesis.
   b. specifying the test statistic.
   c. indicating the *df* or, in the case of *z*, the sample size, *N*, set off in parentheses.
   d. stating the calculated value of the test statistic.
   e. indicating the probability, **p**, of obtaining the calculated value on the basis of chance.

   In a formal research report the results of the statistical test performed on the collected data on children's IQ scores would read as follows:

   > The statistical analysis supports the belief that the selected sample of 36 children does not represent a random sample from a population with a mean IQ score equal to 100 and a standard deviation equal to 15, $z(36) = 2.0$, $p = 0.0456$.

Application Exercises

1. Assume that the time it takes rats to run a maze is normally distributed with a mean (μ) equal to 65 seconds and a standard deviation (σ) equal to 8 seconds. A researcher believes that if the rats' diet is changed their maze running time may also change. A random sample of 100 rats is given a different diet for one month and the times it takes the rats to run the maze at the end of the month is recorded and averaged for the group. The average time ($\bar{X}$) equals 63 seconds. Does changing the diet affect the maze running times of rats?

   Determine

   a. whether reference is made to descriptive or inferential statistics.

   b. whether reference is made to samples, populations, or both. If samples, specify size; if populations, specify whether they are finite or infinite.

   c. the sampling distribution that must be considered to answer the question.

  d. the expected value of the sampling distribution.

  e. the standard error of the sampling distribution.

  f. a general decision rule with respect to the question posed.

  g. the critical values that would define critical regions based on $\alpha = 0.01$.

  h. the critical values that would define critical regions based on $\alpha = 0.05$.

  i. why a nondirectional statistical hypothesis would be formed.

  j. why a two-tailed statistical test would be used.

2. In *Application Exercise 1* the question asked was "Does changing the diet affect the maze running times of rats?" Answer that question by applying the following steps.

  a. State the research hypothesis.

  b. State the null and alternative hypotheses.

  c. Perform a statistical test by doing the following:
    (1) Identify the test statistic and its formula.

    (2) Select alpha.

(3) State a specific decision rule.

(4) Calculate the value of the test statistic.

(5) Determine the probability of obtaining the calculated value of the test statistic for a two-tailed test.

d. Evaluate H_0.

e. Reach a decision about the research hypothesis.

f. State your conclusion about the research hypothesis as you would in a formal research report.

MEETING THE CHALLENGE OF STATISTICS

The following problems pertain to the memory experiment described in the *Meeting the Challenge of Statistics* section in Chapter 1, pages 9-10, of this workbook.

The number of syllables or words correctly recalled by the freshmen in each set of experimental and control groups reproduced from Chapter 1 are as follows:

Nonsense Syllables
Experimental: 12, 13, 11, 11, 9, 10, 13, 12, 12, 10
Control: 10, 11, 9, 9, 6, 11, 6, 5, 8, 8

Emotionally Neutral Words
Experimental: 12, 14, 13, 10, 14, 15, 11, 13, 16, 15
Control: 10, 11, 12, 8, 9, 9, 9, 8, 11, 9

Emotion Laden Words (pleasant, **unpleasant)**
Experimental: (9,**6**), (10,8), (9,7), (8,8), (7,6), (9,7), (10,6), (8,**5**), (7,8), (9,**9**)
Control: (7,**5**), (9,**5**), (6,5), (7,6), (8,7), (7,7), (6,7), (9,**4**), (6,**5**), (5,7)

The mean and standard deviation of the control subjects ($N = 30$), computed from the raw scores, are 10.2 and 2.49, respectively. *Assuming that these are also the values of the population parameters, μ and σ, respectively, do the following:*

1. Determine the expected value of the sampling distribution of the mean for samples of size 30.

2. Determine the standard error of the sampling distribution for samples of size 300.

3. Assuming that the experimental treatment may have altered the characteristic of interest to such a degree that the thirty subjects undergoing the experimental treatment may no longer be considered a random sample from the population represented by the control subjects (*research hypothesis*), form the null and alternative hypotheses.

4. Evaluate the null hypothesis by

   a. identifying a test statistic and its formula.

   b. stating a specific decision rule for $\alpha = 0.05$.

   c. calculating a test statistic.

d. determining the probability for a two-tailed test that the value of the test statistic would be obtained on the basis of chance if the experimental subjects constitute a random sample from the population represented by the control subjects (*use Appendix Table 4*).

5. Reach a decision about H_0.

6. On the basis of your evaluation of H_0, reach a decision about the research hypothesis.

7. Report the results of your statistical test in relation to your evaluation of H_0 and your answer to problem 6.

CHAPTER 11
EVALUATING HYPOTHESES AND ESTIMATING PARAMETERS USING THE t-DISTRIBUTION: THE ONE SAMPLE t-TEST

DETAILED TEXTBOOK OUTLINE

Chapter 11

KEY TERMS AND DEFINITIONS

CI A symbol used to represent confidence interval.

confidence interval An interval that has a certain probability of containing the true value of the population parameter.

confidence interval limits The critical *t*-score values expressed in relation to a sample mean and $s_{\bar{x}}$ that define the smallest and largest estimated values of μ.

effect size The minimal difference between the true mean (μ) and the hypothesized mean (μ_0) expressed in standard deviation units, $(\mu - \mu_0)/\sigma$, that an investigator wishes to detect when evaluating statistical hypotheses.

hypothesis testing A procedure used to evaluate the null and alternative hypotheses about a specific population involving information obtained from a sample or samples.

interval estimation A procedure used to determine intervals likely to contain (usually with a probability of 0.95) the value of a specified parameter.

lower limit of a confidence interval The smallest value in a confidence interval used to estimate μ.

μ_0 The symbol used for the *hypothesized* value of a population mean.

N - 1 Degrees of freedom for the one-sample *t*-statistic where *N* equals sample size.

95 percent confidence interval A range of values that has a probability of 0.95 of containing μ.

one-sample *t*-statistic A test statistic used when $\sigma_{\bar{x}}$ is estimated from the data of a sample to evaluate a statistical hypothesis when μ is hypothesized or to estimate a range of values for μ when μ is not hypothesized.

Chapter 11

parametric statistics A variety of test statistics based on theoretical distributions whose use requires that certain assumptions, including assumptions about the parameters of the populations from which the observed samples or samples were obtained, be true.

point estimation A procedure whereby a single value for a population parameter is estimated from sample data.

sample element A term used to refer to a member of a sample.

$s_{\bar{x}}$ The symbol used to represent the estimate of the standard error of the mean.

$s_{\bar{x}} = s/\sqrt{N}$ The formula used to obtain a value for the estimate of the standard error of the mean where s is an estimate of the population standard deviation and N = sample size.

t-distribution A family of theoretical sampling distributions. The shape of each specific t-distribution changes as a function of sample size.

t-statistic A statistic used to test a hypothesis about the expected value of a sampling distribution and to determine intervals that are likely to contain the expected value.

$t = (\bar{X} - \mu_0)/s_{\bar{x}}$ The formula for the one-sample t-statistic.

upper limit of the confidence interval The largest value in a confidence interval used to estimate μ.

$\bar{X} - t_{table}(s_{\bar{x}})$ The formula used to calculate the lower limit of a confidence interval.

$\bar{X} + t_{table}(s_{\bar{x}})$ The formula used to calculate the upper limit of a confidence interval.

MASTERING THE LANGUAGE OF STATISTICS

Fill-in-the Blanks

Write the appropriate term(s) in the space(s) provided.

Researchers use inferential statistics for estimating _____ or _____ and for _____ _____. _____ _____ is the procedure whereby a single value for a population is estimated from sample data. _____

_____ is the procedure by which information obtained from a sample is used to determine intervals likely to contain the values of a specified parameter. _____ _____, on the other hand, is a procedure by which information obtained from a sample can be used to evaluate hypotheses about the population from which the sample was selected. When the hypotheses about the population are statements about parameters, the type of statistics used to evaluate the hypotheses are called _____ statistics. _____ statistics are based on theoretical distributions whose use in evaluating hypotheses requires that certain assumptions about the population be true. One such statistic, the ____-_____, is used to test hypotheses about the expected value of a sampling distribution and to determine intervals that are likely to contain the expected value. These intervals are called _____ _____. The values that define the limits of these intervals are called _____ _____ _____. The _____ _____ _____ define the smallest and largest estimates of the specified parameter. The smallest value in the confidence interval is called the _____ _____ of the confidence interval; the largest value is called the _____ _____ of the confidence interval. The _____ _____ confidence interval is a range of values defined by the _____ and _____ _____ of the confidence interval that has a probability of 0.95 of containing the parameter, μ. The upper and lower limits of the 95% confidence interval can be calculated by applying formulas

_____ and _____, respectively.

The t_{table} in the formulas refer to the value of t in Appendix Table 5 for a specific df with alpha set at 0.05. The specific df used is _____, the size of the sample minus one. The symbol _____ in the formulas represents an estimate of the standard error of the sampling distribution of the mean. The formula used to obtain a value for the estimate of the standard error of the mean is _____.

When the t-statistic is used to evaluate hypotheses about μ, the formula used is _____. In this formula $\bar{X}$ refers to the sample mean, $s_{\bar{x}}$ refers to the estimate of the standard error of the mean, and μ_0 refers to a _____ value of μ. The minimal difference between μ and μ_0 that an investigator wishes to detect when evaluating hypotheses about μ is called _____ _____. Effect size, _____, is expressed in standard deviation units.

True-False Items

Place a T for true or an F for false in the space provided before each item.

1.____ Point estimation refers to a procedure by which a range of values for a population parameter is estimated from sample data.

2.____ Parametric statistics used for estimation and hypothesis testing are based on theoretical distributions.

3.____ The t-statistic is a parametric statistic.

4.____ Interval estimation is a procedure by which information obtained from a sample is used to evaluate hypotheses about a specific population.

5.____ The one-sample t-statistic is a test statistic used to evaluate hypotheses when μ is hypothesized and $\sigma_{\bar{x}}$ is known.

Chapter 11

6.____ Sample element refers to a sample member.

7.____ μ_0 refers to a hypothesized value for the mean of the population.

8.____ The degrees of freedom for the one-sample t-statistic are $N - 1$.

9.____ The minimal distance between μ and μ_0 is called the hypothesized difference.

10.____ Effect size is expressed in standard deviation units.

11.____ Intervals that have a certain probability of containing the true value of a population parameter are called probability intervals.

12.____ Values that define a confidence interval are called confidence interval limits.

Multiple-Choice Items

Blacken out the letter corresponding to the correct answer.

1. The procedure whereby a single value for a population parameter is estimated from sample data is called
   (a) hypothesis testing.
   (b) point estimation.
   (c) interval estimation.
   (d) parametric statistics.

2. The procedure whereby information obtained from sample data is used to evaluate hypotheses about a specific population is called
   (a) hypothesis testing.
   (b) point estimation.
   (c) interval estimation.
   (d) parametric statistics.

3. A test statistic used to evaluate hypotheses about the expected value of a sampling distribution when μ is estimated and $\sigma_{\bar{x}}$ is estimated is
   (a) μ_0.
   (b) μ.
   (c) t.
   (d) $s_{\bar{x}}$.

4. A sample element is a
   (a) statistic.
   (b) member of a sample.
   (c) measure of a sample characteristic.
   (d) measure of a population characteristic.

5. The formula for the one-sample t-statistic is
   (a) $(\bar{X} - \mu)/s_{\bar{x}}$.
   (b) $(\bar{X} - \mu)/\sigma_{\bar{x}}$.
   (c) $(\bar{X} - \mu_0)/s_{\bar{x}}$.
   (d) $(\bar{X} - \mu_0)/\sigma_{\bar{x}}$.

6. The minimal difference between μ and μ_0 in standard deviation units that an investigator wishes to detect is called
   (a) effect size.
   (b) a confidence interval.
   (c) a critical value.
   (d) the upper limit of a confidence interval.

7. Estimating values of effect size can be accomplished by using
   (a) values for parameters obtained from published research.
   (b) one's personal beliefs.
   (c) special conventions.
   (d) all of the above.

8. A range of scores that have a certain probability of containing the true value of a population parameter is called
   (a) effect size.
   (b) a confidence interval.
   (c) a critical range.
   (d) all of the above.

9. The 95 percent confidence interval refers to
   (a) a range of scores that has a 95% chance of containing the true value of μ.
   (b) an interval that has a 95% chance of not containing the true value of μ.
   (c) an interval that has no chance of containing μ.
   (d) effect size.

10. The formula for the upper limit of the 95% CI is
    (a) $\bar{X} - t_{table}(s_{\bar{x}})$.
    (b) $\mu_0 - t_{table}(s_{\bar{x}})$.
    (c) $\bar{X} + t_{table}(s_{\bar{x}})$.
    (d) $\mu_0 + t_{table}(s_{\bar{x}})$.

11. The degrees of freedom for the one-sample t-statistic is symbolized
    (a) t.
    (b) N.
    (c) $N - 1$.
    (d) $N - 2$.

12. μ_0 is the symbol for
    (a) the population mean.
    (b) the sample mean.
    (c) a hypothesized value for the population mean.
    (d) a hypothesized value for the sample mean.

APPLYING STATISTICAL CONCEPTS

Example Application

An experimenter found that monkeys would solve a puzzle if it were put into their cage. Even though they were not reinforced by the experimenter for solving puzzles, after experience with several puzzles, the monkeys solved puzzles on the average in thirty seconds. The experimenter then wanted to see if a food reward (external reinforcement) for solving puzzles would alter the puzzle-solving behavior of the monkeys. There could be several possible outcomes: (1) the monkeys would continue to solve puzzles at the same rate, (2) the monkeys would solve puzzles faster since, according to the *law of effect*, a reinforcer can strengthen any behavior, and (3) the monkeys would solve puzzles slower because external reinforcement would interfere with intrinsic (self-generated) motivation. The experimenter tests a random sample of 16 monkeys and finds the mean puzzle solving time to be 32 seconds with a standard deviation of 2 seconds. Assuming that the 30-second puzzle-solving average in the absence of external reinforcement is typical of the population of monkeys, is the 32-second mean puzzle-solving time evidence that external reinforcement alters the puzzle-solving behavior of monkeys?
    The material in this and the two preceding chapters indicates that to answer this question you should state the **research hypothesis**, translate the research hypothesis into a testable **statistical hypothesis**, choose a **test statistic**, and perform a **statistical test**. The research hypothesis is that external reinforcement will alter the puzzle-solving behavior of the monkeys. This hypothesis is translated into the **nondirectional statistical alternative hypothesis**, H_1: $\mu_{external\ reinf.} \neq 30$. The alternative hypothesis is negated to form the **null hypothesis**, H_0: $\mu_{external\ reinf.} = 30$. The test statistic to use is the **one-sample t-statistic** since the mean of the population is hypothesized to be 30 ($\mu_0 = 30$), and the standard error of the mean ($s_{\bar{x}}$) must be estimated from the sample data. The formula for the one-sample t-statistic is $(\bar{X} - \mu_0)/s_{\bar{x}}$. In this case $\mu_0 = \mu_{external\ reinf.} = 30$; $\bar{X} = 32$, and $s_{\bar{x}} = 2/\sqrt{16} = 0.5$. In performing the statistical test set the **significance level** ($\alpha = 0.05$) and determine a **decision rule**. Since the **degrees of freedom** for the one-sample t-statistic is $N - 1$, the decision rule is **reject H_0 if $|t_{calc}| \geq 2.13$**. This value is found by looking up the value of t_{table} in Appendix Table 5 for $\alpha = 0.05$

and $df = 15$. By substituting the appropriate values in the t formula, $t = (32 - 30)/0.5 = 4.00$. Since 4.00 is greater than 2.13, reject H_0. It can be concluded that giving external reinforcers to monkeys for solving puzzles does alter their puzzle solving time. In this case, it slows their puzzle solving time, $t(15) = 4.00$, $p < 0.05$.

The experimenter can now establish a **confidence interval** for $\mu_{external\ reinf.}$. To establish the **95 percent confidence interval** use the t_{table} value stated in the decision rule (2.13). The formula for the **upper limit** of the confidence interval is $\bar{X} + t_{table}(s_{\bar{x}})$. The value for the upper limit is $32 + 2.13(0.5) = 33.06$. The formula for the **lower limit** of the confidence interval is $\bar{X} - t_{table}(s_{\bar{x}})$. The value for the lower limit is $32 - 2.13(0.5) = 30.94$. Formally expressed, the 95% confidence interval for $\mu_{external\ reinf.}$ is given as **95% *CI*: $30.94 \le \mu \le 33.06$**.

Application Exercises

1. A developmental psychologist familiar with the outcome of the experimenter's research on monkeys in the *Example Application* wants to see if external reinforcement will also alter intrinsically motivated behavior of children. Over a long period of time the psychologist observes the behavior of children enrolled in a large nursery school class. These observations indicate that the children spend approximately four hours over a two-week period coloring with crayons and that this activity is a self-selected activity. From this population of children the psychologist then selects a sample of children by picking from a jar, one at a time, thoroughly mixed slips of paper on which the name of each child was written. Over the next two weeks of nursery school, the psychologist reinforces the coloring behavior of the sample of children with little trinkets that they can keep. At the end of the two weeks, the psychologist stops reinforcing their coloring behavior and records the amount of time each child in the sample spends coloring for the next two weeks of nursery school. The amount of time to the nearest 0.1 hour each child spent coloring over that two week period is as follows: 4.1, 3.7, 3.9, 3.8, 3.5, 3.9, 4.0, 4.1, 3.7, 3.6, 3.4, 4.0, 3.8, 3.5, 3.5, 3.6.

    Determine

    a. whether reference is made to descriptive or inferential statistics.

    b. the population and whether it is finite or infinite

    c. the type of sample (random, randomized, or biased).

    d.   the mean of the sample.

    e.   the standard deviation of the sample.

    f.   the sampling distribution that would be used to determine the 95% confidence interval for the mean of the population from which the sample was drawn.

    g.   an estimate of the standard error of the sampling distribution.

    h.   the upper limit of the 95% confidence interval.

    i.   the lower limit of the 95% confidence interval.

    j.   the formal expression of the confidence interval.

2.   Did the reinforcement in *Application Exercise 1* alter the intrinsically motivated coloring behavior of the children?

   Answer this question by

   a.   stating the research hypothesis.

b. translating the research hypothesis into an alternative hypothesis, H_1.

c. negating the alternative hypothesis to form the null hypothesis, H_0.

d. selecting a test statistic.

e. specifying the degrees of freedom.

f. setting a significance level.

g. forming a decision rule.

h. calculating the value of the test statistic.

i. evaluating the null hypothesis on the basis of the calculated test statistic and the decision rule.

j. reaching a conclusion about the research hypothesis based on your evaluation of H_0.

k. stating the outcome of your test as you would in a formal report.

Chapter 11

MEETING THE CHALLENGE OF STATISTICS

The following problems pertain to the memory experiment described in the *Meeting the Challenge of Statistics* section in Chapter 1, pages 9-10, of this workbook. The number of nonsense syllables correctly recalled by the freshmen in the experimental group reproduced from Chapter 1 are as follows:

Nonsense Syllables
Experimental: 12, 13, 11, 11, 9, 10, 13, 12, 12, 10

1. The mean of the control group presented nonsense syllables is 8.3. This value is an unbiased estimate of the μ of the population from which this control group was selected. Assume 8.3 is, in fact, the mean number of nonsense syllables recalled by the population of individuals not going to sleep within an hour after learning the list of nonsense syllables to one perfect recitation. If going to sleep immediately after learning the list has an effect on retention as measured by the number of nonsense syllables recalled, then the mean of the population from which the experimental group was selected should not equal 8.3.

   Test the hypothesis that the mean of the population from which the experimental group presented nonsense syllables was selected is also 8.3 by

   a. stating the research hypothesis based on the information given above.

   b. translating the research hypothesis into an alternative hypothesis, H_1.

   c. negating the alternative hypothesis to form the null hypothesis, H_0.

   d. selecting a test statistic.

   e. specifying the degrees of freedom.

  f. setting a significance level.

  g. forming a decision rule.

  h. calculating the value of the test statistic.

  i. evaluating the null hypothesis on the basis of the calculated test statistic and the decision rule.

  j. reaching a conclusion about the research hypothesis based on your evaluation of H_0.

  k. stating the outcome of your test as you would in a formal report.

2. Confidence intervals are generally determined when an investigator is not likely to have a hypothesized value for μ.

Establish the 95% confidence for the mean of the population from which the experimental group presented nonsense syllables was selected by

    a.   computing the upper limit of the 95% confidence interval.

    b.   computing the lower limit of the 95% confidence interval.

    c.   formally expressing the 95% CI.

3. Although most behavioral scientists use the 95% CI, a 99% confidence interval is sometimes desired.

   Establish the 99% confidence interval for the mean of the population from which the experimental group presented nonsense syllables was selected by

    a.   computing the upper limit of the 99% confidence interval.

    b.   computing the lower limit of the 99% confidence interval.

    c.   formally expressing the 99% CI.

CHAPTER 12
TESTS FOR TREATMENT EFFECTS ON TWO INDEPENDENT SAMPLES

DETAILED TEXTBOOK OUTLINE

Chapter 12

KEY TERMS AND DEFINITIONS

F-statistic   A parametric statistic for determining whether the variances of two populations are homogeneous based on observations obtained from two random independent samples.

$F = s^2_{larger}/s^2_{smaller}$ Formula used to determine F where s^2 is calculated for both samples and the larger variance is used as the numerator and the smaller variance is used as the denominator.

Mann-Whitney *U*-test   A nonparametric test that is used when the conditions for the *t*-test for two independent samples are not met.

$N_1 + N_2 - 2$ Formula for calculating the *df* for the *t*-statistic used with two random independent samples.

nonparametric statistical tests   Tests used when population parameters are not hypothesized in H_0 and H_1 and no assumptions are made about the form of the population distributions from which the samples are selected.   The statistical hypothesis evaluated with nonparametric statistical tests is that the population distributions are not different.

sampling distribution of the difference between two means   A theoretical distribution based on the difference between the means of all possible pairs of random samples of given sizes selected from a population.

s_{diff} Symbol for the *estimate* of the standard error of the sampling distribution of the difference between two means.

$s_{diff} = \sqrt{s^2_p/N_1 + s^2_p/N_2}$ Formula for calculating an estimate of the standard error of the sampling distribution of the difference between two means.

s^2_p Symbol for the pooled estimate of the population variance obtained from two random independent samples.

$s^2_p = [(N_1 - 1)s^2_1 + (N_2 - 1)s^2_2]/[(N_1 - 1) + (N_2 - 1)]$ Formula for calculating a value for the pooled estimate of the population variance.

σ_{diff} Symbol for the standard error of the sampling distribution of the difference between means.

$\sigma_{diff} = \sqrt{\sigma_1^2/N_1 + \sigma_2^2/N_2}$ Defining equation for the standard error of the theoretical sampling distribution of the difference between means.

t-test for two random independent samples A parametric test used to determine if there is a significant difference between the means of two random independent samples.

$t = [(\bar{X}_1 - \bar{X}_2) - \mu_{diff}]/s_{diff}$ Equation for the t-statistic for two random independent samples where μ_{diff} is the hypothesized expected value stated in the null hypothesis.

$t = (\bar{X}_1 - \bar{X}_2)/s_{diff}$ Formula used for calculating a value for t for two random independent samples.

μ_{diff} The symbol for the expected value of the sampling distribution of the difference between means.

$\mu_{diff} = \mu_1 - \mu_2$ Defining equation of the expected value of the sampling distribution of the difference between means.

$U_1 = N_1N_2 + [N_1(N_1 + 1)]/2 - R_1$ and $U_2 = N_1N_2 + [N_2(N_2 + 1)]/2 - R_2$ Formulas for calculating the value for the Mann-Whitney U-statistic where the smaller of the two U-values is used to evaluate the null hypothesis.

MASTERING THE LANGUAGE OF STATISTICS

Fill-in-the-Blanks

Write the appropriate term(s) in the space(s) provided.

This chapter extends the discussion of the t-test by

introducing the ___-____ for two _____ _____

samples, a parametric test used to determine if there is a

significant difference between the means of two random

independent samples. One assumption underlying this test is

the assumption of homogeneity of variance, an assumption that

is generally tested with the _____ statistic. The ___-

_____ is a parametric statistic used to determine if the

variances of two populations are the same or different based

on observations made on independent samples of each
population. It is calculated by the formula:

_____.

When data are collected from two random independent
samples, the ___-_____ and its theoretical sampling
distribution are used to evaluate statistical hypotheses about
the means. This theoretical distribution is known as the
sampling distribution of the _____ _____ _____
_____. The expected value of this theoretical
distribution, symbolized as _____, is equal to the
difference between the population means from which the samples
are randomly selected. The defining equation for μ_{diff} is
_____. The standard error of the sampling
distribution of the difference between two means, symbolized,
_____, is defined by the following equation:
_____. Since investigators rarely have values
for μ_1, μ_2, σ_1, and σ_2, they hypothesize a value for _____
and estimate a value for _____. The ___-_____ is then
calculated by subtracting _____ from $\bar{X}_1 - \bar{X}_2$, and dividing by
_____, the estimate of the standard error of the sampling
distribution of the _____ _____ _____ _____.
The defining equation for the *t*-statistic
is:_____. Since _____ is generally hypothesized
to be zero, the *t*-formula is most often written as:
_____. A value for s_{diff} is calculated by the
following formula_____. The symbol, _____, refers
to the pooled estimate of the population variance. The

procedure for pooling the variance is indicated in the

following formula: _____. The

t-distribution, you will recall, is a family of distributions

based on ____, the degrees of freedom. The *df* for the two-

sample *t*-statistic is _____.

If the conditions of the *t*-test are not met, then a

_____ _____ test must be used to make

inferences about the populations from which the samples were

selected. When using _____ _____ tests, no

assumptions are made about the specific shape of the

population distribution(s) and no parameters are hypothesized.

The nonparametric statistical test generally used when the

conditions of the *t*-test are not met is called the _____-

_____ ____-_____. The *U*-statistic is calculated by

the following formulas: U_1 = _____; U_2 =

_____.

True-False Items

*Place a T for true or an F for False in the space provided
before each item.*

1.____ The Mann-Whitney *U*-test is a parametric test used to
determine if two population distributions differ.

2.____ Parametric tests make no assumptions about population
parameters.

3.____ The *t*-test for two random independent samples is a
test used to determine if there is a significant
difference between the means of two random independent
samples.

4.____ The *F*-statistic is a nonparametric statistic.

5.____ $\sigma_{diff} = \sigma_1 - \sigma_2$.

Chapter 12

6.____ $F = (\sigma^2_{smaller}) / (\sigma^2_{larger})$.

7.____ The value of μ_{diff} is generally greater than zero.

8.____ The pooled estimate of the population variance is symbolized s^2_p.

9.____ The df used with the t-test for two random independent samples is $N_1 + N_2 - 2$.

10.____ The larger of the two U's, U_1 and U_2, is used to evaluate the H_0 for the Mann-Whitney U-test.

11.____ The value for $\overline{X}_1 - \overline{X}_2$ in the t-formula is generally hypothesized.

12.____ The t-statistic is a parametric statistic for determining whether the variance of two populations are homogeneous based on observations obtained from two random independent samples.

Multiple-Choice Items

Blacken out the letter corresponding to the correct answer.

1. The t-test for two random independent samples
   (a) makes no assumptions about the specific shape of the population distribution(s).
   (b) does not require hypothesizing parameters.
   (c) requires five conditions be met.
   (d) is a parametric statistical test used to determine if the variances of two populations are homogeneous.

2. The ____ statistic is a parametric statistic used to determine if the variances of two populations are homogeneous.
   (a) U
   (b) t
   (c) z
   (d) F

3. The numerator of the F-ratio used to test the assumption of homogeneity of variance is
   (a) the smaller of the two sample variances.
   (b) the larger of the two sample variances.
   (c) the difference between the two sample variances.
   (d) the sample variance divided by the df.

4. The standard error of the sampling distribution of a difference between two means is symbolized
   (a) $\sigma_1 - \sigma_2$.
   (b) $s_1 - s_2$.
   (c) σ_{diff}.
   (d) s_{diff}.

5. The symbol s_p^2 refers to the
   (a) standard error of the sampling distribution of a difference between two means.
   (b) population variance.
   (c) the pooled sample variance.
   (d) the pooled population variance.

6. The *df* for the *t*-test for two random independent samples is
   (a) $N_1 + N_2 - 2$.
   (b) $N - 1$.
   (c) $N - 2$.
   (d) $N_1 + N_2 + 2$.

7. The estimate of the standard error of the sampling distribution of a difference between two means is
   (a) s.
   (b) $s_1 - s_2$.
   (c) $\sigma_1 - \sigma_2$.
   (d) s_{diff}.

8. $\mu_1 - \mu_2$ equals
   (a) zero.
   (b) μ_{diff}.
   (c) the expected value of the sampling distribution of the mean.
   (d) all of the above.

9. $\mu_1 - \mu_2$ is generally hypothesized to be
   (a) larger than $\bar{X}_1 - \bar{X}_2$.
   (b) smaller than $\bar{X}_1 - \bar{X}_2$.
   (c) equal to $\bar{X}_1 - \bar{X}_2$.
   (d) none of the above.

10. $(\bar{X}_1 - \bar{X}_2)/s_{diff}$ is the
    (a) defining equation for the *t*-statistic.
    (b) formula for calculating a value for the two-sample *t*-statistic.
    (c) test of the assumption of homogeneity of variance.
    (d) formula for calculating the estimate of the standard error of the sampling distribution of the difference between two means.

11. The Mann-Whitney U-test
    (a) is a parametric test.
    (b) makes an assumption about the specific shape of the population distribution(s).
    (c) does not require hypothesizing values for parameters.
    (d) tests the hypothesis: $\mu_1 - \mu_2 = 0$.

12. In performing the Mann-Whitney U-test, the smaller of the U-values
    (a) does not need to be computed.
    (b) is used to make a decision about H_0.
    (c) must be larger than U_{table}.
    (d) is not used as the U-statistic.

APPLYING STATISTICAL CONCEPTS

Example Application

A classic problem in the psychology of learning is whether or not an animal can learn a response without responding. For example, can an animal learn a maze without actually walking or running through the maze? The answer to this question would depend upon what you believe animals are learning in the maze situation. If you believe that in a maze situation animals are learning a muscular response, then if no response is permitted no maze learning will occur. If, on the other hand, you believe that in a maze situation what is crucial is learning what stimulus leads to what other stimulus, then if such relationships can be perceived in the absence of muscular responding, learning will occur. To obtain a solution to the problem experimentally, two randomized groups of hungry rats were "trained" in a maze in which food was available in the goal box. One group of rats was permitted to run or walk through the maze. The other group was restrained in a little cart and pulled through the maze by the experimenter. Both groups of rats were then given five nonreinforced test trials during which they were allowed to run or walk through the maze freely. The total errors made during the five trials were recorded and are as follows:

Walk or run: 10, 9, 10, 11, 11, 10, 11, 12, 12, 13.
Pulled in cart: 12, 11, 15, 16, 14, 13, 12, 15, 14, 13.

Since the data are collected from two random independent samples, and the F-statistic, $F = s^2_{larger}/s^2_{smaller} = 2.5/1.43 = 1.75$, does not lead to a rejection of the hypothesis, $H_0: \sigma_1^2 = \sigma_2^2$, the t-statistic and its theoretical sampling distribution, the **sampling distribution of the difference between two means**, are used to evaluate statistical hypotheses about the means. The expected value of this sampling distribution, μ_{diff}, is hypothesized to be zero, that is, $\mu_{diff} = \mu_1 - \mu_2 = 0$. The standard error of the sampling distribution is estimated from the pooled sample variance, s_p^2, by the following formula:

$$s_{diff} = \sqrt{\frac{s_p^2}{N_1} + \frac{s_p^2}{N_2}}$$

where $\quad s_p^2 = \dfrac{(N_1 - 1)\, s_1^2 + (N_2 - 1)\, s_2^2}{(N_1 - 1) + (N_2 - 1)}$

Assuming that the experimenter believes that the two different "training" procedures will result in different outcomes, the alternative hypothesis is written as H_1: $\mu_1 - \mu_2 \neq 0$, or $\mu_{diff} \neq 0$. The null hypothesis, the negation of H_1, is, as mentioned previously, H_0: $\mu_{diff} = 0$. The specific decision rule with alpha = 0.05 and $df = N_1 + N_2 - 2 = 18$ is:

If $|t_{calc}| \geq 2.10$, reject H_0.

The evaluation of H_0 requires calculating the **t-statistic** by the following formula:

$$t = \frac{\overline{X}_1 - \overline{X}_2}{s_{diff}}$$

In this example $t = (10.9 - 13.5)/1.40 = -1.86$. Because the absolute value of t_{calc} is less than t_{table} as specified in the decision rule, H_0 is not rejected. There is no evidence to support the experimenter's belief that the two "training" procedures result in different outcomes, $t(18) = -1.86$, $p > 0.05$.

The **Mann-Whitney U-test**, a **nonparametric test**, can also be applied to the maze data since the samples are random independent samples and the data are collected along a ratio scale. In order to perform the Mann-Whitney U-test, the data from both samples must be ranked collectively, and the ranks must be summed. Two U-values are then calculated with the following formulas:

$$U_1 = N_1 N_2 + \frac{N_1 (N_1 + 1)}{2} - R_1$$

$$U_2 = N_1 N_2 + \frac{N_2 (N_2 + 1)}{2} - R_2$$

The *smaller* of the two U-values is used to evaluate the null hypothesis. For this example the ranks and U's are as follows:

Walk or run
 Data: 9, 10, 10, 10, 11,   11, 11,   12,   12, 13
 Rank: 1, 3, 3, 3, 6.5, 6.5, 6.5, 10.5, 10.5, 14

Cart
 Data: 11,   12,   12, 13, 13,   14,   14,   15,   15, 16
 Rank: 6.5, 10.5, 10.5, 14, 14, 16.5, 16.5, 18.5, 18.5, 20

$$U_1 = 10(10) + 10(11)/2 - 64.5 = 90.5$$
$$U_2 = 10(10) + 10(11)/2 - 145.5 = 9.5.$$

The general decision rule for the Mann-Whitney U-statistic is:

$$\text{If } U_{calc} \leq U_{table}, \text{ then reject } H_0.$$

In this example, for samples of size $N = 10$ and alpha set at 0.05, $U_{table} = 23$. The H_0, the population distributions do not differ, is therefore rejected. The results of this test support the experimenter's belief, **$U(10,10) = 9.5$, $p < 0.05$.** Surprisingly, the Mann-Whitney U-test leads to a different conclusion than the two-sample t-statistic. Ordinarily, when the conditions of the t-test for two random independent samples are satisfied, the t-test has a greater power and is the preferred test.

Application Exercises

1. One concept of drive or motivation is that it is an energizer of behavior. It is possible, however, that a drive like the hunger drive could weaken a behavior because it results from removing a source of energy. To see if the hunger drive energizes or weakens a motor response in rats, an experimenter randomly divides a group of 20 rats into two groups of 10. One group is deprived of food for 12 hours; the other group has free access to food during the same 12-hour period. At the end of the 12 hours both groups have access to a running wheel for 0.5 hour. The wheel revolutions made by the rats in each group are as follows:

   Deprived: 150, 125, 110, 120, 130, 135, 135, 135, 140, 135
   Nondeprived: 125, 100, 85, 95, 105, 110, 115, 110, 110, 110.

   Determine

   a. the mean of each group.

    b.   the variance of each group.

    c.   if the data fail to support the assumption of homogeneity of variance.

    d.   the research hypothesis.

    e.   the alternative and null hypotheses.

    f.   the appropriate test statistic based on the answer to part *c*.

    g.   the specific decision rule for alpha set at 0.05.

    h.   the value of the test statistic.

    i.   the decision about H_0.

    j.   what the decision about H_0 means in terms of the research hypothesis expressed formally as in a research report.

2. *Latent learning* refers to learning that is not demonstrated in performance at the time it occurs. In the laboratory it most often occurs in the absence of reward. To see if the absence of reward during maze training would interfere with learning or lead to latent learning in rats, an animal behaviorist gives two randomized groups of rats 10 training trials in a complex maze. Both groups are deprived of food for six hours before each training trial. Training trials occur at the rate of one per day for 10 days. One group is rewarded with food each time it reaches the goal box on a training trial; the other group is not given the food reward. A test trial is given on the eleventh day. Just before their test trials the animals are placed in the goal box and given a food reward. The number of errors made on the test trial is the measure recorded (see accompanying data). There are three possible outcomes: (1) nonreward leads to more maze exploration, latent learning occurs, and the nonrewarded group makes fewer errors on the test trial; (2) nonreward leads to more maze exploration, latent learning occurs, and the nonreward group performs the same as the reward group; (3) nonreward does not lead to more maze exploration and latent learning and the nonreward group makes more errors on the test trail than the reward group.

Reward: 1, 10, 3, 7, 8, 7, 6, 5, 7, 2, 11, 9
Nonreward: 10, 10, 11, 12, 9, 9, 8, 10, 10, 11, 9, 10

Determine

a. the mean of each group.

b. the variance of each group.

    c. if the data fail to support the assumption of homogeneity of variance.

    d. the research hypothesis.

    e. the alternative and null hypotheses.

    f. the appropriate test statistic based on the answer to part *c*.

    g. the specific decision rule for alpha set at 0.05.

    h. the value of the test statistic.

    i. the decision about H_0.

    j. what the decision about H_0 means in terms of the research hypothesis expressed formally as in a research report.

Chapter 12

MEETING THE CHALLENGE OF STATISTICS

The following problems pertain to the memory experiment described in the *Meeting the Challenge of Statistics* section in Chapter 1, pages 9-10, of this workbook. The number of syllables or words correctly recalled by the freshmen in each set of experimental and control groups reproduced from Chapter 1 are as follows:

Nonsense Syllables
Experimental: 12, 13, 11, 11, 9, 10, 13, 12, 12, 10
Control: 10, 11, 9, 9, 6, 11, 6, 5, 8, 8

Emotionally Neutral Words
Experimental: 12, 14, 13, 10, 14, 15, 11, 13, 16, 15
Control: 10, 11, 12, 8, 9, 9, 9, 8, 11, 9

Emotion Laden Words (pleasant, **unpleasant)**
Experimental: (9,**6**), (10,**8**), (9,**7**), (8,**8**), (7,**6**), (9,**7**),
(10,**6**), (8,**5**), (7,**8**), (9,**9)**
Control: (7,**5**), (9,**5**), (6,**5**), (7,**6**), (8,**7**), (7,**7**), (6,**7**),
(9,**4**), (6,**5**), (5,**7**).

Ignoring the different types of verbal material, such as nonsense syllables,

1. state an appropriate research hypothesis.

2. test for heterogeneity of variance in the experimental and control populations.

3. state the alternative and null hypotheses.

4. on the basis of the answer to part *2* select an appropriate test statistic to evaluate H_0.

5. form a decision rule.

6. calculate a value for the test statistic.

7. reach a decision about H_0 on the basis of the calculated value of the test statistic and the decision rule.

8. state your conclusion about the outcome of the experiment as you would in a formal research report.

CHAPTER 13
TESTS FOR TREATMENT EFFECTS ON TWO DEPENDENT SAMPLES

DETAILED TEXTBOOK OUTLINE

Chapter 13

KEY TERMS AND DEFINITIONS

before-after or **pretest-posttest design** Experimental design in which the dependent variable is measured for sample elements before and after introduction of the independent variable.

covariance A measure of the tendency for scores of corresponding members of dependent samples to covary. The adjusted average of products of the deviation scores for corresponding members of dependent samples.

D Symbol for the difference between scores of corresponding members of dependent samples.

$\bar{D}$ (pronounced "D-bar") Symbol for the mean of the difference scores for corresponding members of dependent samples.

dependent samples *t*-test A parametric test to determine if there is a significant difference between the means of treatment populations from which two dependent samples are drawn.

genetic factors Factors resulting from a common heredity that have the potential to influence measures of the dependent variable.

matching A procedure of forming groups in such a way that each sample member has a member in the other sample with which it is identical or highly similar on a characteristic that could potentially influence measures of the dependent variable.

matching by premeasuring the dependent variable The procedure of assigning subjects to samples in such a way that for each sample member there is a member in the other sample with the same or highly similar measure of the characteristic of interest.

mutual category A characteristic or set of characteristics that are shared by individuals or elements and that have the potential to influence measures of the dependent variable.

repeated measures The procedure of measuring the dependent variable for each sample member under each treatment condition.

s_{cov}^2 Symbol for the covariance of samples 1 and 2.

$s_{cov}^2 = \sum (X - \bar{X})(Y - \bar{Y})/(N - 1)$ Defining equation for covariance.

$s_{cov}^2 = [\Sigma XY - (\Sigma X)(\Sigma Y)/N]/(N - 1)$ Computational formula for the covariance.

$s_{diff} = \sqrt{\dfrac{s_p^2 - s_{cov}^2}{N_1} + \dfrac{s_p^2 - s_{cov}^2}{N_2}}$ Formula for the standard error of a difference between the means of dependent samples.

$s_{diff} = \sqrt{s_D^2/N}$ Formula for the standard error of a difference between means of dependent samples computed from difference scores for corresponding sample members.

$t = \overline{D}/\sqrt{s_D^2/N}$ Formula for the dependent samples t-test that uses difference scores to compute the standard error of the difference between means.

T The smaller absolute value of the sums of signed ranks computed in the Wilcoxon Matched-Pairs Signed-Ranks test.

Wilcoxon Matched-Pairs Signed-Ranks test A nonparametric test of treatment effects on two dependent samples.

MASTERING THE LANGUAGE OF STATISTICS

Fill-in-the-Blanks

Write the appropriate terms(s) in the space(s) provided.

Dependence in sampling can be achieved by _____ or

_____ _____. _____ refers to the procedure of

forming samples in such a way that each sample member has a

member in the other sample with which it is identical or highly

similar on a characteristic that could potentially influence

measures of the dependent variable. _____ _____

requires measuring the dependent variable for a sample member

under each treatment condition. Matching can be by either

_____ _____, _____ _____, or _____.

Chapter 13

A _____ _____ refers to a characteristic or set of characteristics that are shared by a class of individuals or elements that have the potential to influence measures of the dependent variable in an experiment. _____ _____ are factors resulting from a common heredity that have the potential to influence measures of the dependent variable. Matching by _____ the dependent variable is the procedure of assigning subjects to samples in such a way that for each sample member there is a member in the other sample with the same or highly similar measure of the characteristic of interest. With respect to _____ _____, if the measures are taken before and after the introduction of the independent variable in an experiment, the design is often referred to as a _____-_____ or _____-_____ design.

By using dependent samples, an investigator can compute and remove variation, called _____, due to the unique features of sample members. A measure of _____ is the adjusted average of the products of deviation scores for the corresponding members of dependent samples. It is symbolized _____. The defining equation for covariance is _____. An algebraic manipulation of the defining equation yields _____, the formula for computing a value for covariance. Once covariance is computed, it can be subtracted from the pooled sample variance to compute the standard error of the difference between the means of dependent samples as follows:_____.
Alternatively, s_{diff} can be computed using difference scores,

184

Chapter 13

symbolized _____, by the following formula:_____. Once s_{diff} has been calculated, a value of the test statistic, t, can be obtained by the following formula: _____. In the formula, _____ refers to the mean of the difference scores.

As with the independent samples t-test, the _____ _____ ___-_____ requires that the conditions of normality and homogeneity of variance be met and that the measures of the dependent variable are measured on an interval or ratio scale. If any one of these conditions are not met, the nonparametric test called the _____ _____-_____ _____-_____ test should be used. The _____ _____- _____ _____-_____ test is a nonparametric test of treatment effects on two dependent samples. The test statistic for the Wilcoxon Matched-Pairs Signed-Ranks test is symbolized _____ and is the smaller absolute value of the sums of the signed ranks. The decision rule for the Wilcoxon _____ statistic is: If $|T_-|$ of $|T_+| \leq T_{table}$, then reject H_0.

True-False Items

Place a T for true or an F for false in the space provided before each item.

1. ____ Genetic factors are factors resulting from a common heredity that have the potential to influence the independent variable.

2. ____ A mutual category refers to a characteristic or set of characteristics that are shared by a class of individuals or elements and that have the potential to influence measures of the dependent variable.

3. ____ Matching by premeasuring the dependent variable is the procedure of assigning subjects to samples in such a way as to ensure independent sampling.

4. ____ When measures are taken on sample members before and

after introduction of the independent variable in an experiment, the experimental design is often referred to as a before-after design.

5.____ When measures are taken on sample members before and after introduction of the independent variable in an experiment, the experimental design is often referred to as a pretest-posttest design.

6.____ Covariance refers to variation in the dependent measures due to the unique features of sample members.

7.____ Covariance is a measure of the tendency for scores of corresponding sample members of dependent samples to covary.

8.____ A measure of covariance is the adjusted average of the products of the scores for corresponding sample members of dependent samples.

9.____ The parametric test used to test for a difference between the means of dependent samples is the Wilcoxon Matched-Pairs Signed-Ranks test.

10.____ The Wilcoxon test statistic is symbolized t.

11.____ The Wilcoxon test statistic is the smaller absolute value of the summed ranks.

12.____ $\bar{D}$ is the symbol for the difference scores in the parametric test of the difference between the means of two dependent samples.

Multiple-Choice Items

Blacken out the letter corresponding to the correct answer.

1. The dependent samples t-test is a
   (a) nonparametric test to determine if there is a significant difference between the means of treatment populations from which two dependent samples are drawn.
   (b) nonparametric test of treatment effects on two dependent samples.
   (c) parametric test to determine if there is a significant difference between the means of treatment populations from which two dependent samples are drawn.
   (d) parametric test to determine if there is homogeneity of variance in the population distributions from which two random dependent samples are selected.

2. Covariance is
   (a) a measure of the tendency for scores of corresponding members of dependent samples to covary.

   (b) the adjusted average of the products of deviation scores
       for corresponding members of dependent samples.
   (c) variation in the dependent measures due to the unique
       features of sample members.
   (d) all of the above.

3. Matching by putting one animal from each of 10 pairs of
   littermates in the experimental group and the other
   littermates in the control group would be by
   (a) mutual category.
   (b) genetic factors.
   (c) premeasurement.
   (d) repeated measures.

4. A pretest-posttest design involves
   (a) matching by a mutual category.
   (b) matching by genetic factors.
   (c) matching by premeasurement.
   (d) repeated measures.

5. If students' attitudes toward drinking alcohol are measured
   before and after viewing a movie on the devastating effects
   of alcohol on family life, dependence in sampling is
   achieved by
   (a) matching by a mutual category.
   (b) matching by genetic factors.
   (c) matching by premeasurement.
   (d) by repeating measures.

6. The test statistic T is used to determine
   (a) if two population distributions differ.
   (b) if the means of two populations from which dependent
       samples were drawn differ.
   (c) if there is dependence in sampling.
   (d) if there is heterogeneity of variance.

7. $\bar{D}$ is the symbol for
   (a) the mean of the difference scores.
   (b) the Wilcoxon test statistic.
   (c) the parametric dependent samples test statistic.
   (d) a difference score.

8. D is the symbol for
   (a) the sum of sign ranks.
   (b) the lower sum of signed ranks.
   (c) the Wilcoxon test statistic.
   (d) a difference score.

9. $\bar{X} - \bar{Y}$ is equivalent to
   (a) t.
   (b) T.
   (c) $\bar{D}$.
   (d) D.

10. The symbol D̄ is used in computing
    (a) D̄.
    (b) t.
    (c) T.
    (d) all of the above.

11. A before-after design involves
    (a) matching by a mutual category.
    (b) matching by genetic factors.
    (c) matching by premeasurement.
    (d) repeated measures.

12. t is the symbol for
    (a) the parametric test statistic that tests for
        homogeneity of variance in the measures made on members
        of two dependent samples.
    (b) the nonparametric test statistic that tests for a
        difference between the means of dependent samples.
    (c) the Wilcoxon Matched-Pairs Signed-Ranks test statistic.
    (d) dependent samples t-test.

APPLYING STATISTICAL CONCEPTS

Example Application

When doing research with animals, it is often necessary to cross
foster offspring. Cross fostering means that Mother A's
offspring will be raised by Mother B, and Mother B's offspring
will be raised by Mother A. A question that can be asked is do
mothers treat foster offspring differently than they treat their
natural offspring. To answer this question, each of ten rat
litters was culled to four males and four females at
parturition. Two males and two females from each litter were
replaced by two males and two females from a different litter so
that each mother rat cared for two male and two female natural
offspring and two male and two female foster offspring. When
the rat pups were six days old, the home nest was attached to an
"open field", a barren three foot square enclosure, which the
mother rat could enter. Each of the eight rat pups were placed
one at a time on two different occasions in the center of the
open field. The number of rat pups of each kind (natural,
foster) that were returned by the mother to the nest within a 2-
minute test period was the dependent measure.
    If you understand the material in the *Ways of Achieving
Dependence in Sampling* section of Chapter 13 of the textbook,
you know that dependency in sampling was achieved by **repeated
measures**. You also know that either the **dependent samples t-
test** or the **Wilcoxon Matched-Pairs Signed-Ranks test** can be used
to analyze the data from the experiment. Since the data
collected are measured along a ratio scale, you know that, if
the conditions of normality and homogeneity of variance are met,

the **dependent samples *t*-test** is appropriate. If either of these conditions are not met, then the **Wilcoxon test statistic, *T*,** would be most appropriate. If the **dependent samples *t*-test** is appropriate, the standard error of the sampling distribution of a difference between means can be estimated by using the computed **covariance, s^2_{cov},** or by using difference scores (**D**). Assume the accompanying data (X, Y) in Table 13.1 from the experiment meet the assumptions of normality and homogeneity of variance.

Table 13.1   Data and Calculations Used for Example Application of Analysis of Data Obtained for Dependent Samples

| Mother (Litter) | Sample 1 Foster | | Sample 2 Natural | | Product | (X − Y) | | (+) | (−) |
	X	X²	Y	Y²	XY	D	D²	Ranks	Ranks
1	4	16	3	9	12	1	1	+1.5	
2	5	25	5	25	25	0			
3	8	64	4	16	32	4	16	+7.5	
4	2	4	4	16	8	−2	4		−3.5
5	2	4	3	9	6	−1	1		−1.5
6	7	49	3	9	21	4	16	+7.5	
7	6	36	4	16	24	2	4	+3.5	
8	8	64	5	25	40	3	9	+5.5	
9	7	49	2	4	14	5	25	+9.0	
10	6	36	3	9	18	3	9	+5.5	
Σ =	55	347	36	138	200	19	85	+40.0	−5.0

$$s^2_{foster} = [347 - 55^2/10]/9 = 4.94 \quad s^2_{natural} = [138 - 36^2/10]9 = 0.93$$

$$s^2_D = [85 - 19^2/10]/9 = 5.43$$

The research hypothesis is that mother rats will treat foster offspring differently than they treat their natural offspring. Translating this hypothesis into an alternative hypothesis gives H_1: $\mu_{foster} \neq \mu_{natural}$. Negating H_1 yields the null hypothesis, H_0: $\mu_{foster} = \mu_{natural}$. The test statistic is the **dependent samples *t*-statistic** and the general decision rule is:

If $|t_{calc}| \geq t_{table}$, then reject H_0.

For alpha set at 0.05 and df = $N - 1$ = 9, the specific decision rule is:

If $|t_{calc}| \geq 2.26$, then reject H_0.

The estimate of the standard error of the difference between means, s_{diff}, is calculated using the covariance, s^2_{cov}, and pooled variance, s^2_p as follows:

$$s^2_{cov} = [\Sigma XY - (\Sigma X)(\Sigma Y)/N]/(N - 1) =$$
$$[200 - (55)(36)/10]/9 = 0.22$$

$$s^2_p = [(N_1 - 1)s^2_1 + (N_2 - 1)s^2_2]/[(N_1 - 1) + (N_2 - 1)] =$$
$$[9(4.94) + 9(0.93)]/[9 + 9] = 2.935$$

$$s_{diff} = \sqrt{\frac{s^2_p - s^2_{cov}}{N} + \frac{s^2_p - s^2_{cov}}{N}}$$

$$s_{diff} = \sqrt{\frac{2.935 - 0.22}{10} + \frac{2.935 - 0.22}{10}} = 0.74$$

The value for t is then calculated by the following formula:

$$t = \frac{\overline{X} - \overline{Y}}{s_{diff}} = \frac{5.5 - 3.6}{0.74} = 2.57$$

Since t_{calc} (2.57) is greater than t_{table} (2.26), reject H_0. Rejecting H_0 lends support to the research hypothesis. These results would be expressed formally in a research report as follows: **The results support the hypothesis that rat mothers treat foster offspring differently than they treat natural offspring, $t(9) = 2.57$, $p < 0.05$.**
A value for t could also have been calculated using difference scores (D) as follows:

$$t = \frac{\overline{D}}{\sqrt{\frac{s^2_D}{N}}} = \frac{1.9}{\sqrt{\frac{5.43}{10}}} = 2.57$$

Difference scores are also used in calculating T, the **Wilcoxon Matched-Pairs Signed-Ranks statistic.** The absolute values of the difference scores, excluding zero, are ranked from lowest to highest with tied scores being given the average of the corresponding ranks. The sign (+,-) of the difference score is then affixed to its rank. The positive and negative ranks are then summed independently. The T-statistic is the smaller absolute value of the summed ranks. If $|T_-|$ or $|T_+| \leq T_{table}$, then reject H_0: The population distributions do not differ. In our example the absolute value of T_- is 5.0 and T_{table} is 6.0 for alpha set at 0.05 and N, the number of signed ranks, equal to 10. The null hypothesis is, therefore, rejected.

Application Exercises

Chapter 13

1. A group of college sophomores was selected to participate in a study of experimenter bias by putting slips of paper with the names of all the sophomores at the college in a drum, thoroughly mixing them, and drawing out the names one at a time until eight names were selected. Each sophomore was asked to train two rats on a complex maze. Although the two rats given to each student were selected at random from the college rat colony, the students were told that one of the rats was a superior maze learner while the other rat was an inferior maze learner. Each rat was to be given training trials with an intertrial interval of two minutes until it made five consecutive errorless trials, the learning criterion. The number of training trials required by the rats to reach this criterion (excluding the 5 criterion trials) was recorded and are as follows:

Student	1	2	3	4	5	6	7	8
Rat Group								
Inferior (X)	13	11	10	13	10	15	10	13
Superior (Y)	8	10	11	9	10	12	8	10

Determine

   a. the population of interest.

   b. whether the sample(s) is(are) random, randomized, or biased.

   c. if the sample(s) is(are) independent, dependent, or neither.

   d. the method of achieving dependence in sampling, if applicable.

   e. the independent variable and its levels.

   f. the dependent variable.

    g. an operational definition of the dependent variable.

    h. the dependent measure.

    i. an organization of the data similar to that of Table 13.1 without the variance calculations.

_____

_____

_____

_____

_____

_____

_____

_____

_____

_____

_____

_____

_____

_____

    j. the mean and variance for the trials to criterion of the "superior" rats.

    k. the mean and variance for the trials to criterion of the "inferior" rats.

2. For the data presented in *Application Exercise 1* assume the population distributions are normally distributed and there is homogeneity of variance.

   Determine

   a. an appropriate nondirectional research hypothesis.

   b. the alternative hypothesis.

   c. the null hypothesis.

   d. the appropriate test statistic.

   e. the decision rule for alpha set at 0.05.

   f. the covariance of the X- and Y-scores.

   g. a value for s_p^2.

   h. a value for the estimate of the standard error of the difference between means using the measure of covariance and s_p^2.

i. a value for the test statistic using s_{diff} obtained in part h of this exercise.

j. a value for t using difference scores.

k. what should be concluded about H_0.

l. what your decision about H_0 means in terms of the research hypothesis.

m. how the results would be presented in a research report.

n. A value for the Wilcoxon Matched-Pairs Signed-Ranks statistic.

o. the null hypothesis tested by the Wilcoxon test.

p. the decision rule for the Wilcoxon test.

q. whether H_0 should be rejected or not on the basis of your answer to part *n* of this exercise.

r. how the results would be presented in a formal research report.

MEETING THE CHALLENGE OF STATISTICS

The following problems pertain to the memory experiment described in the *Meeting the Challenge of Statistics* section in Chapter 1, pages 9-10, of this workbook. The data to be used for these problems follow:

Emotion Laden Words (pleasant, **unpleasant)**

Experimental: (9,**6**), (10,**8**), (9,**7**), (8,**8**), (7,**6**), (9,**7**), (10,**6**), (8,**5**), (7,**8**), (9,**9**)

Control: (7,**5**), (9,**5**), (6,**5**), (7,**6**), (8,**7**), (7,**7**), (6,**7**), (9,**4**), (6,**5**), (5,**7**)

1. Organize the data of the experimental group's recall of pleasant and unpleasant words in a fashion similar to Table 13.1 to perform the calculations necessary to determine a value of the *t*-test for dependent samples using difference scores. Note: The Columns X^2, Y^2, and XY are not necessary.

_____
_____
_____
_____
_____
_____
_____
_____
_____
_____
_____
_____

2. Determine the mean for the pleasant words of the experimental group.

3. Determine the mean for the unpleasant words of the experimental group.

4. Using difference scores, determine a value for t of the experimental group's scores for pleasant and unpleasant words recalled.

5. Symbolize H_0 and reach a conclusion concerning it.

6. Tell what your decision about H_0 means in terms of the appropriate research hypothesis as you would in a formal research report.

7. Organize the data of the control group's recall of pleasant and unpleasant words in a fashion similar to Table 13.2 to perform the calculations necessary to determine a value of the *T*-test for dependent samples using Wilcoxon Matched-Pairs Signed-Ranks test.

_____
_____
_____
_____
_____
_____
_____
_____
_____
_____
_____
_____
_____
_____

8. Perform the Wilcoxon Matched-Pairs Signed-Ranks test on the data from the control group.

9. State the null hypothesis tested by the Wilcoxon test.

10. State the decision rule for the Wilcoxon test at the 5% level of significance.

11. Reach a conclusion about an appropriate research hypothesis as you would in a formal research report.

CHAPTER 14
COMPLETELY RANDOMIZED DESIGNS AND THE ONE-WAY ANALYSIS OF VARIANCE

DETAILED TEXTBOOK OUTLINE

Chapter 14

KEY TERMS AND DEFINITIONS

analysis of variance (ANOVA) A parametric test used to test a hypothesis about means for any number of treatment levels ($k \geq 2$).

ANOVA Acronym for analysis of variance.

a posteriori or *post hoc test* A test used to make unplanned comparisons of means, that is, comparisons that were not planned prior to collecting the data.

a priori test A test used to make planned comparisons of means, that is, comparisons that are decided on in the planning stages of the experiment.

between-group degrees of freedom The number of groups minus one.

between-group estimate of σ^2 Group size (n) times the variance of the means divided by the number of groups minus one. The between-group sum of squares divided by the between-group degrees of freedom.

199

between-group mean square The adjusted average of the deviations of the sample means from the mean of all the scores.

between-group sum of squares The sample size times the sum of the squared deviations of the sample means from the grand mean.

completely randomized designs A class of experimental designs in which there are two or more treatment levels of a single independent variable.

critical value The smallest absolute value of a mean difference that will lead to a rejection of the null hypothesis, $H_0: \mu_j = \mu_{j'}$.

CR-k The symbol for a completely randomized design in which there are k-independent samples.

CV The symbol for critical value.

$CV = \sqrt{F_{table} [MS_{wg}(1/n_j + 1/n_{j'})]}$ Critical value for the *a priori* F-test for making comparisons between means.

degrees of freedom The number of deviations minus the number of points about which the deviations are taken.

df_{bg} The symbol for between-group degrees of freedom.

$df_{bg} = k - 1$ The formula for computing the between-group degrees of freedom.

df_{tot} The symbol for the total degrees of freedom.

$df_{tot} = nk - 1$ The formula for computing the total degrees of freedom when sample sizes are equal.

$df_{tot} = N_{tot} - 1$ The formula for computing total degrees of freedom when sample sizes are unequal.

df_{wg} The symbol for within-group degrees of freedom.

$df_{wg} = k(n - 1)$ The formula for computing within-group degrees of freedom when sample sizes are equal.

$df_{wg} = N_{tot} - k$ The formula for computing within-group degrees of freedom when sample sizes are unequal.

F-distribution Theoretical distribution of the ratio of two variances.

$F = MS_{bg}/MS_{wg}$ Formula for obtaining F in the one-way ANOVA.

$F = (\bar{T}_j - \bar{T}_{j'})^2/MS_{wg}(1/n_j + 1/n_{j'})$ The formula for obtaining F in the *a priori* F-test.

F_{max} The ratio of the largest variance to the smallest variance when there are more than two levels of an independent variable.

$F_{max} = s^2{}_{largest}/s^2{}_{smallest}$ Formula used to compute F_{max}.

F-ratio or **F in the one-way ANOVA** Ratio of the between-group mean square to the within-group mean square.

G The grand total; the symbol for the sum of all scores obtained in the experiment.

$\bar{G}$ (pronounced "G-bar") The grand mean; the symbol for the mean of all the scores obtained in the experiment.

grand mean Mean of all the scores obtained in the experiment.

grand sum Sum of all the scores obtained in the experiment.

j The subscript used to denote a specific ($j = 1, 2, 3, \ldots k$) treatment or group.

k The symbol used to denote the number of treatment levels or groups in a completely randomized design.

Kruskal-Wallis one-way ANOVA by ranks A nonparametric test used to determine if k independent samples come from different populations, where $k \geq 2$.

$K\text{-}W$ The symbol for the statistic obtained in the Kruskal-Wallis one-way ANOVA by ranks.

$K\text{-}W = [12/\{N_{tot}(N_{tot} + 1)\}]\Sigma(R^2{}_j/n_j) - 3(N_{tot} + 1)$ The formula used to obtain the statistic for the Kruskal-Wallis one-way ANOVA by ranks.

leptokurtic The term used to refer to a distribution that is extremely peaked in appearance.

mean square Variance in the ANOVA; the adjusted average of the squared deviations from the mean.

monomial An expression consisting of one term.

MS The symbol for mean square.

MS_{bg} The symbol for the between-group mean square.

$MS_{bg} = SS_{bg}/df_{bg}$ The formula used to compute the between-group mean square.

MS_{wg} The symbol for the within-group mean square.

$MS_{wg} = SS_{wg}/df_{wg}$ The formula used to compute the within-group mean square.

$\mu_1 = \mu_2 = \mu_3 = \ldots = \mu_k$ The symbolized null hypothesis for the parametric one-way ANOVA.

n The symbol for the number of scores in a group.

n_j The symbol for the number of scores in a specific ($j = 1, 2, 3, \ldots k$) group.

N_{tot} Symbol for the total number of obtained scores when group sizes are not equal.

null hypothesis for the parametric one-way ANOVA A statement that the means of the population from which the samples were drawn are equal.

one-way ANOVA The analysis of variance used to analyze the data generated by a *CR-k* experiment.

pairwise comparisons Comparisons between any two groups in an experimental design involving two or more groups.

planned comparisons The comparisons one decides to make in the planning stages of an experiment.

platykurtic The term used to refer to a distribution that is extremely flat in appearance.

R_j The symbol for the sum of the ranked scores of a specific ($j = 1, 2, 3, \ldots k$) treatment group.

$$s_p^2 = \frac{(N_1 - 1)s_1^2 + (N_2 - 1)s_2^2 + \ldots + (N_k - 1)s_k^2}{N_1 + N_2 + \ldots + N_k - k}$$ The formula for computing the pooled variance of k independent samples.

SS The symbol for the sum of squares used in the parametric one-way ANOVA.

SS_{bg} The symbol for the between-group sum of squares.

$SS_{bg} = n[\Sigma(\bar{T}_j - \bar{G})^2]$ The defining equation for the between-group sum of squares.

$SS_{bg} = (3) - (1) = \Sigma T_j^2/n - G^2/nk$ The computational formula for the between-group sum of squares.

SS_{tot} The symbol for the total sum of squares.

$SS_{tot} = \Sigma(X - \bar{G})^2$ The defining equation for the total sum of squares.

$SS_{tot} = (2) - (1) = \Sigma X^2 - G^2/nk$ The computational formula for the total sum of squares.

SS_{wg} The symbol for the within-group sum of squares.

$SS_{wg} = \Sigma SS_j = \Sigma[\Sigma(X - \bar{T}_j)^2]$ The defining equation for the within-group sum of squares.

$SS_{wg} = (2) - (3) = \Sigma X^2 - \Sigma T^2_j/n$ The computational formula for the within-group sum of squares.

sum of squares   The term given to the sum of the squared deviations from the mean in the parametric one-way ANOVA.

T_j The symbol for the sum of the scores for a specific ($j = 1, 2, 3, \ldots k$) treatment group.

$\bar{T}_j$ (pronounced "T_j-bar")   The mean of the scores of a specific ($j = 1, 2, 3, \ldots k$) treatment group.

total sum of squares   The sum of the squared deviations of all the obtained scores from the mean of all the scores.

unplanned comparisons   Comparisons used to explore the data to find out the source of significance of the F in ANOVA.

within-group degrees of freedom   The sum of the degrees of freedom for the individual treatment groups.

within-group estimate of σ^2   The within-group sum of squares divided by the within-group degrees of freedom.

within-group mean square   The name given to the within-group estimate of σ^2.

within-group sum of squares   The sum of the sums of squares of the individual treatment groups.

MASTERING THE LANGUAGE OF STATISTICS

Fill-in-the-Blanks

Write the appropriate term(s) in the space(s) provided.

Chapter 14

The class of designs called _____ _____ designs

is symbolized _____ -___ , where _____ must be equal to or

greater than two and represents the number of treatment levels

of a single independent variable. The parametric analysis used

to test a hypothesis about means for any number of treatment

levels is called the _____ ____ _____ . The

acronym for analysis of variance is _____ . Because the *CR-k*

design involves a single independent variable, the ANOVA used to

analyze the data generated by a *CR-k* experiment is called the

_____-_____ ANOVA. The null hypothesis for the one-way

ANOVA is, _____ . You test this hypothesis

by examining the ratio of the _____-_____ estimate of

σ^2 to the _____-_____ estimate of σ^2. This ratio is

the familiar ___-_____ .

In the ANOVA, the sum of the squared deviations from the

mean is called the _____ ___ _____ and is symbolized

_____ . The *SS* used in obtaining the within-group estimate of σ^2

is called the _____-_____ _____ ___ _____ and is

symbolized _____ . Similarly, the *SS* used in obtaining the

between-group estimate of σ^2 is called the _____-_____

_____ ____ _____ and is symbolized _____ . A third sum

of squares, called _____ _____ ___ _____ and symbolized

_____ , is defined as the sum of the squared deviations of all

the obtained scores from the mean of all the scores, called the

_____ _____ and symbolized _____ . The grand mean is

obtained by dividing the sum of all the scores, called the

_____ _____ and symbolized _____ , by the total number of

204

scores, symbolized _____, when the sample size (designated ____)
is the same for all groups and symbolized _____ when samples
sizes are unequal.

Variance in the ANOVA is called _____ _____,
symbolized _____, and refers to the adjusted average of squared
deviations from the mean. The mean square, symbolized _____,
is obtained by dividing SS by the _____ ___ _____,
symbolized _____. Thus, the within-group mean square,
symbolized _____, is obtained by dividing SS_{wg} by _____, the
within-group degrees of freedom. Similarly, _____ is obtained
by dividing SS_{bg} by _____. The ___-_____ in the one-way ANOVA
is the ratio of MS_{bg} to MS_{wg}.

The defining equation and computational formula for SS_{tot} are
_____ and _____,
respectively. The equation $\Sigma SS_j = \Sigma[\Sigma(X - \bar{T}_j)^2$ is the defining
equation for _____, where ____ refers to the sum of the
scores for a specific treatment group. The corresponding
computational formula for SS_{wg} is _____.
The defining equation for the _____-_____ sum of squares is
_____$= n[\Sigma(\bar{T}_j - \bar{G})^2$; the corresponding computational formula is
_____. The degrees of freedom for the between-
group, within-group, and total sources of variation are obtained
by these three formulas, respectively, _____, _____
or _____, and _____ or _____. The mean square for
a specific source is obtained by dividing the SS by its
corresponding df as shown in the following formulas: $MS_{wg} =$
_____ and $MS_{bg} =$ _____. A value for F is then obtained

by the following ratio: _____. A significant *F* in the ANOVA
on the data from an experiment in which *k* > 2 directs you to
further analyze the data. The tests used to further analyze the
data depend upon decisions made during the planning stage of the
experiment. If, in planning the experiment, you decide that
there are certain mean comparisons that you will make, the
comparisons are called _____ comparisons and the tests
you would use are called __ _____ tests. If, on the other
hand, no specific comparisons are planned, comparisons made
following ANOVA are called _____ and require ___
_____ or _____ _____ tests. The
following __ _____ *F*-test is used for making _____
comparisons: _____. When *n*'s are equal and
the number of _____ comparisons, that is comparisons
between two groups, is large, it is preferable to obtain a
_____ value, symbolized _____, which is the smallest
absolute difference between $\bar{T}_j$ and $\bar{T}_{j'}$ that can be considered
significant at the preset level of significance. The formula
for obtaining a critical value is:

_____.

If the conditions underlying the parametric one-way ANOVA
are not met such as the population distributions being extremely
flat or _____, extremely peaked or _____,
or exhibiting heterogeneity of variance as detected by the _____
test, then the _____-_____ _____-_____ _____ __
_____ is a nonparametric test that can be used to determine if *k*
random independent samples come from different populations. The

206

Chapter 14

test statistic for the Kruskal-Wallis test is ___-___ and is obtained by the following formula:

_____ .

True-False Items

Place a T for true or an F for false in the space provided before each item.

1. ____ In the symbol $CR-k$, k represents the number of independent variables.

2. ____ $CR-k$ designs involve only a single independent variable.

3. ____ $\Sigma SS_j = SS_{wg}$.

4. ____ The formula for computing df_{tot} is $nk - 1$.

5. ____ The F-ratio in the one-way ANOVA is the ratio of the within-group mean square to the between-group mean square.

6. ____ $SS_{tot} = MS_{bg} + MS_{wg}$.

7. ____ Tests called *a priori* tests are used for making planned comparisons.

8. ____ *Post hoc* tests and *a priori* tests are the same.

9. ____ Critical value refers to the level of significance.

10. ____ If the F_{max} test indicates that you are to reject the hypothesis of homogeneity of variance, then the parametric one-way ANOVA would be an appropriate analysis to perform on the data.

11. ____ The Kruskal-Wallis one-way ANOVA by ranks is a nonparametric test that is used to determine if k random independent samples come from different populations.

12. ____ The Kruskal-Wallis test statistic is symbolized $K-W$.

Multiple-Choice Items

Blacken out the letter corresponding to the correct answer.

1. In the symbol for completely randomized designs, $CR-k$ the k represents
   (a) the number of class intervals.
   (b) the number of independent variables.
   (c) the number of levels of the independent variable.

    (d) the number of dependent measures.

2. The null hypothesis for the parametric one-way ANOVA states
    (a) that all the means are equal.
    (b) that the population distributions do not differ.
    (c) that the means are not all equal.
    (d) that the population distributions differ.

3. The between-groups degrees of freedom is
    (a) the number of groups times the sample size minus one.
    (b) the total number of scores minus one.
    (c) the number of groups minus one.
    (d) $nk - 1$.

4. The group size times the sum of the squared deviations of
the group means from the grand mean is
    (a) the within-group sum of squares.
    (b) the total sum of squares.
    (c) the within-group estimate of σ^2.
    (d) the between-group sum of squares.

5. The total degrees of freedom equal
    (a) $N_{tot} - 1$.
    (b) $(nk - k) + (k - 1)$.
    (c) $nk - 1$.
    (d) all of the above.

6. The within-group sum of squares equals
    (a) ΣSS_j.
    (b) $\Sigma[\Sigma(X - \bar{T}_j)^2]$.
    (c) $\Sigma X^2 - \Sigma T_j^2/n$.
    (d) all of the above.

7. Tests made on planned comparisons are called
    (a) prehoc tests.
    (b) post hoc tests.
    (c) *a priori* tests.
    (d) *a posteriori* tests.

8. The statistic F_{max} is used to test the hypothesis
    (a) that the population distributions do not differ.
    (b) that the means of the population distributions do not
        differ.
    (c) that the population variances do not differ.
    (d) that $\mu_1 = \mu_2$.

9. The smallest absolute difference between two treatment means
that can be considered significant for a given alpha is
called
    (a) the critical difference.
    (b) the critical value.
    (c) the significant difference.
    (d) the alpha level.

10. Leptokurtic refers to a distribution that
    (a) is extremely peaked.
    (b) is extremely flat.
    (c) is symmetrical.
    (d) is normally distributed.

11. The symbol (2), as decribed in the text, equals
    (a) ΣX^2.
    (b) $\Sigma (X - \bar{G})^2$.
    (c) G^2 / nk.
    (d) ΣT^2_j.

12. A nonparametric test statistic used to determine if k
    independent random samples come from different populations
    is
    (a) F_{max}.
    (b) MS_{bg} / MS_{wg}.
    (c) K–W.
    (d) F.

APPLYING STATISTICAL CONCEPTS

Example Applications

1. A learning psychologist believes that the quality of
   reinforcement will have an effect on resistance to
   extinction of a learned response. Resistance to extinction
   is operationally defined as the number of times a response
   is made after reinforcement has been withdrawn. Three
   groups of rats are randomly selected from the university rat
   colony. Each animal is housed in an operant conditioning
   chamber, a small enclosure that has a bar protruding from
   one wall which operates a food mechanism. Each time the bar
   is depressed, a food pellet is automatically made available
   to the animals in a small cup. All rats have free access to
   water and are permitted 100 food pellets before
   reinforcement is withdrawn. For one group of rats the food
   pellets are made of plain flour and water (basic
   reinforcer). For another group the flour food pellets
   contain citric acid (low quality reinforcer). For the
   remaining group, the food pellets contain saccharin (high
   quality reinforcer). After the food reinforcement is
   withdrawn, the animals are permitted to remain in the
   chamber for two hours and the number of bar depressions made
   in the two hour period is recorded. The accompanying table
   (Table 14.1) shows the data for the three groups.

Table 14.1
The Number of Bar Depressions, X, (Squared Bar Depressions, X^2, and Summary Statistics) Made by Three Differentially Reinforced (Basic, Low Quality, High Quality) Groups of Rats during the Two Hour Period after Food Reinforcement Was Withdrawn (N = 5 per Group)

Basic		Low Quality		High Quality	
X	X^2	X	X^2	X	X^2
95	9025	79	6421	110	12100
85	7225	80	6400	100	10000
88	7744	84	7056	99	9801
98	9604	87	7569	98	9604
97	9409	75	5625	101	10201

$T_j = 463$ 405 508 $G = 1376$
$\overline{T}_j = 92.6$ 81.0 101.6
$T_j^2/n = 42873.8$ 32805.0 51612.8
$s_j^2 = 33.3$ 21.5 23.3

$\Sigma X^2 = 127,784$

Since there are more than two levels of a single independent variable, analysis of these data require the application of a **one-way ANOVA**. Whether a **parametric** or **nonparametric one-way ANOVA** is to be applied depends on whether or not the conditions underlying the parametric one-way ANOVA are met. The data are from randomized independent samples and the dependent measure is along a ratio scale. Assuming bar depressions in the populations which the samples represent are normally distributed, the only condition that remains to be met is the condition of homogeneity of variance. Heterogeneity of variance can be detected with the F_{max}-**test**. The F_{max}-**statistic** is the ratio of the largest variance (s_j^2) to the smallest variance, that is, $F_{max} = s^2{}_{largest}/s^2{}_{smallest} = 33.3/21.5 = 1.55$. Since the calculated value of F_{max} is less than the table value, the hypothesis of homogeneity of variance is not rejected. The parametric one-way ANOVA, then, is appropriate.

To perform the parametric one-way ANOVA on these data values for three computational symbols, **(1)**, **(2)**, and **(3)** must be calculated. The value for **(1)** is $G^2/nk = 126,225.1$. The value for **(2)** is $\Sigma X^2 = 127,784.0$ and the value for **(3)** is $\Sigma T_j^2/n = 42873.8 + 32805.0 + 51612.8 = 127,291.6$. These values are entered in Table 14.2, the **working format** for the parametric one-way ANOVA. Also entered in Table 14.2 are the values for SS_{bg}, SS_{wg}, and SS_{tot} obtained by the following formulas:

$$SS_{bg} = (3) - (1) = 127,291.6 - 126,225.1 = 1066.5,$$
$$SS_{wg} = (2) - (3) = 127,784.0 - 127,291.6 = 492.4,$$
$$SS_{tot} = (2) - (1) = 127,784.0 - 126,225.1 = 1558.9.$$

The value for df and MS in Table 14.2 are obtained by the following formulas:

$$df_{bg} = k - 1 = 3 - 1 = 2; \quad MS_{bg} = SS_{bg}/df_{bg} = 533.25,$$
$$df_{wg} = k(n - 1) = 3(4) = 12; \quad MS_{wg} = SS_{wg}/df_{wg} = 41.00$$
$$df_{tot} = nk - 1 = 15 - 1 = 14.$$

The value for F is then obtained by dividing the MS_{bg} by the MS_{wg}. The value for F is given in Table 14.2.

Since $F_{calc} > F_{table}$ at the 0.05 level of significance, H_0: $\mu_{basic} = \mu_{low\ quality} = \mu_{high\ quality}$ is rejected and the research hypothesis is supported. Formally stated, the results of the experiment indicate that quality of reinforcement has an effect on resistance to extinction of a bar depression response in rats, $F(2,12) = 13.01$, $p < 0.05$.

Table 14.2
Summary Table for ANOVA Performed on the Hypothetical Quality of Reinforcement Data of Table 14.1.

Computational Symbol Values	Source of Variation	SS	df	MS	F
(1) = 126,225.1	Between-Groups	1066.5	2	533.25	13.01
(2) = 127,784.0	Within-Groups	492.4	12	41.00	
(3) = 127,291.6	Total	1558.9	14		

2. Since in *Example Application 1*, the number of levels of the independent variable, k, is greater than two, rejecting H_0 not only tells the investigator that quality of reinforcement is having an effect on resistance to extinction of the bar depression response, but also indicates that further analysis is required. Had the investigator intended to make specific comparisons or all **pairwise comparisons**, the comparisons are **planned comparisons**. Planned comparisons are made with *a priori tests*. Assume the investigator planned to compare the resistance to extinction of rats given the low and high quality reinforcers with that of the rats given the basic reinforcer. An appropriate *a priori* test would be the *F*-test. Following is the formula for F:

$$F = \frac{(\overline{T}_j - \overline{T}_{j'})^2}{MS_{wg}\left(\dfrac{1}{n_j} + \dfrac{1}{n_{j'}}\right)}$$

For the comparison between the means of the low quality and the basic groups,

$$F = \frac{(92.6 - 81)^2}{41.00\left(\frac{1}{5} + \frac{1}{5}\right)} = 8.20$$

Comparing the calculated value of F with the table value in Appendix Table 6 in the textbook for 1 and 12 df at the 0.05 level of significance indicates that H_0: $\mu_{basic} = \mu_{low\ quality}$ should be rejected. The comparison between the means of the basic and high quality groups yields $F = 4.94$. A critical value for the difference between means could also have been determined by the following formula:

$$CV = \sqrt{F_{table}[MS_{wg}(1/n_j + 1/n_{j'})]} = \sqrt{4.75(41.00)(1/5 + 1/5)} = 8.33$$

3. Fifteen subjects were randomly divided into three groups. Each group was taught by a different one of three instructional methods: lecture, discussion, computer tutorial. All subjects were then given a test to determine the effectiveness of the three methods. An ANOVA was then performed on the test scores yielding the accompanying partially completed summary table. You can demonstrate your understanding of the relationships among SS_{bg}, SS_{wg}, and SS_{tot}, among df_{bg}, df_{wg}, and df_{tot}, among SS, df, and MS, and among MS_{bg}, MS_{wg}, and F by completing the table.

Table 14.3
Partially Completed ANOVA Table

Source	SS	df	MS	F
Between Groups	____	____	____	6.00
Within Groups	____	____	3.00	
Total	____	____		

To complete the table, the first thing to do is determine the degrees of freedom from the information given in the problem. Since the 15 subjects were divided into three groups, df_{bg} would equal $k - 1 = 3 - 1 = 2$. Since group sizes are unknown and may be unequal, df_{tot} and df_{wg} equal $N_{tot} - 1 = 15 - 1 = 14$ and $N_{tot} - k = 15 - 3 = 12$, respectively. The MS_{bg} can be calculated to be 18.00 by multiplying MS_{wg} (3.00) by F (6.00) since $F = MS_{bg}/MS_{wg}$. Once an MS-value is obtained or known, the corresponding SS can be calculated by multiplying the MS by its corresponding df since $MS = SS/df$. Thus, SS_{bg} and SS_{wg} each equal 36.00. Once SS_{bg} and SS_{wg} are determined, SS_{total} can be calculated since $SS_{bg} + SS_{wg} = SS_{tot}$. In our example, $SS_{tot} = 36.00 + 36.00 = 72.00$.

4. Assume that the data in Table 14.1 in *Example Application 1* do not come from population distributions that are normally distributed. If such is the case, the **Kruskal-Wallis one-way ANOVA by ranks** would be the most appropriate analysis. Since the collected data are measured along a ratio scale, to obtain a value for the Kruskal-Wallis test statistic, *K-W*, the scores would need to be ranked collectively. The ranks for the data in Table 14.1 are shown in Table 14.4.

Table 14.4
The Number of Bar Depressions, *X*, (and Corresponding Ranks) Made by Three Differentially Reinforced (Basic, Low Quality, High Quality) Groups of Rats during the Two-Hour Period after Food Reinforcement Was Withdrawn (N = 5 per Group)

Basic		Low Quality		High Quality	
X	Rank	X	Rank	X	Rank
95	8	79	2	110	15
85	5	80	3	100	13
88	7	84	4	99	12
98	10.5	87	6	98	10.5
97	9	75	1	101	14
$R_1 = 39.5$		$R_2 = 16$		$R_3 = 64.5$	

A value for *K-W* is obtained by the following formula:

$$K\text{-}W = \frac{12}{N(N + 1)} \sum \frac{R_j^2}{n_j} - 3(N + 1)$$

For the present example,

$$K\text{-}W = \frac{12}{15(15 + 1)} \left(\frac{39.5^2}{5} + \frac{16^2}{5} + \frac{64.5^2}{5} \right) - 3(15 + 1) = 11.76$$

As with the parametric one-way ANOVA, the Kruskal-Wallis ANOVA indicates that the quality of reinforcement has an effect on resistance to extinction of the bar depression response in rats, $K\text{-}W(2) = 11.76$. $p < 0.05$.

Application Exercises

1. An investigator of learning in animals believes that magnitude of reinforcement will have an effect on resistance to extinction of a learned response. Three groups of rats

are randomly selected from a population of rats and each is trained to pull a chain to obtain a food reinforcer. One group of rats receives a small food pellet for each chain pull. The second and third groups receive medium and large pellets, respectively, for each chain pull. After sufficient training, the reinforcer is no longer given for a chain pull and the number of times the rats continue to pull the chain in a 20-minute period is recorded. The experimenter decides during the planning stages of the experiment to make all pairwise comparisons. The data (pulls per minute) are shown in Table 14.5.

Table 14.5
The Number of Chain Pulls per Minute during a Twenty-Minute Extinction Session for Rats Trained with Either Small, Medium, or Large Reinforcers (N = 24)

Small	X^2	Medium	X^2	Large	X^2
8		10		12	
10		9		14	
11		12		13	
9		13		12	
9		10		16	
7		11		15	
10		12		14	
7		9		13	

$T_j =$ $\qquad\qquad\qquad\qquad\qquad\qquad\qquad\qquad\qquad$ $G =$

$\overline{T} =$

$T_j^2/n_j =$

$s_j^2 =$

$\qquad\qquad\Sigma X^2 =$

a. Compute F_{max} using values calculated in Table 14.5 as was done in Table 14.1.

b. Symbolize the null hypothesis for the test for heterogeneity of variance.

c. State the specific decision rule for the test for heterogeneity of variance for alpha set at 0.05.

214

d. Reach a decision about the H_0 in part *b* based on your answer to part *a* and the specific decision rule in part *c*.

e. State the research hypothesis for the experiment described in application exercise 1.

f. Translate the research hypothesis into the appropriate statistical hypothesis.

g. State the null hypothesis that you are testing with the ANOVA in symbols (if appropriate).

h. Calculate values for computational symbols (*1*), (*2*), and (*3*) for a one-way ANOVA.

i. Calculate values for SS_{wg}, SS_{bg}, and SS_{tot}.

j. Perform the *ANOVA* and put the results in a summary table.

Table 14.6

Source	SS	df	MS	F

k. On the basis of the results of the ANOVA, reach a decision about H_0.

l. State what your decision means in terms of the research hypothesis as you would in a formal research report.

m. Make all pairwise comparisons using the *a priori* *F*-test.

n. Establish the critical value for a difference between the means of the three groups.

o. Form a table of absolute differences for all possible pairwise comparisons and determine which means are significantly different.

Table 14.7

2. A psychologist is interested in the effects of three different films on reducing anxiety in snake-phobic college students. The films show either snakes alone, college students handling snakes, or children handling snakes. The dependent variable is the distance each subject is willing to stand from a snake after viewing the particular film. The data are collected from three groups of six subjects each and a parametric one-way ANOVA is performed. Table 14.8 is a partially completed summary table for the ANOVA. Demonstrate your understanding of the relationships among the three SS, among the three df, among SS, df, and MS, and among the MS's and F by completing Table 14.8.

Table 14.8
Summary Table for ANOVA Performed on the Data from Snake-Phobic College Students after Viewing Films Involving Snakes

Source	SS	df	MS	F
Between-Groups	_____	_____	_____	6.00
Within-Groups	_____	_____	_____	
Total	81.00	_____		

3. Three random samples of students selected from a large *Principles of Psychology* class were asked to prepare for exams by using three different studying techniques. One technique was simply to read the textbook material with no mnemonic aids. A second group was asked to read the

textbook material highlighting important aspects of the material. The third group was asked to read the textbook material and take notes on it. At the end of the semester rank in class was considered an indicator of the effectiveness of the methods. The class ranks of the students participating are shown in Table 14.9.

Table 14.9
The Class Ranks of Students Who Prepared for Exams by Reading the Textbook Material with no Mnemonic Aids, with Highlighting Important Material, and with Taking Notes on the Material ($N = 25$)

Read Only	Read and Highlight	Read and Take Notes
40	29	16
32	31	26
27	25	23
38	24	15
35	19	7
30	24	14
28	13	6
	17	5
	33	8

a. State why the Kruskal-Wallis is the most appropriate ANOVA to perform on these data.

b. State the research hypothesis.

c. State the null hypothesis.

d. State the specific decision rule.

e. Calculate a value for $K-W$.

f. On the basis of the decision rule and the value for $K-W$, reach a decision about H_0.

g. State the outcome of the experiment in *reporting format*.

Chapter 14

MEETING THE CHALLENGE OF STATISTICS

The following problems pertain to the memory experiment described in the *Meeting the Challenge of Statistics* section in Chapter 1, pages 9-10, of this workbook.

Table 14.10
The Number of Syllables or Words Correctly Recalled by the Three Experimental Groups Described in *Meeting the Challenge of Statistics* Section in Chapter 1 of This Workbook.

Nonsense Syllables	Emotionally Neutral Words	Emotion Laden Words
12	12	15
13	14	18
11	13	16
11	10	16
9	14	13
10	15	16
13	11	16
12	13	13
12	16	15
10	15	18

1. For the experimental design suggested in table 14.10, state an appropriate research hypothesis.

2. Test the data for heterogeneity of variance. (Show work in Table 14.10)

3. On the basis of your answer to part *2*, give the alternative and null hypotheses in symbols (if appropriate) or in words tested by the ANOVA.

4. On the basis of your answer to part *2*, perform the most appropriate ANOVA. If parametric, put results in a summary table.

5. On the basis of the test statistic in the answer to part *4*, reach a conclusion about the H_0 specified in part *3*.

6. Tell what your decision about H_0 means in terms of the research hypothesis.

7. Give the results of the ANOVA in *reporting format*.

8. If appropriate, establish a *CV* for the differences between means and table of absolute differences for all possible pairwise comparisons, otherwise make all pairwise comparisons using the most appropriate *a priori* test to determine which means differ significantly.

CHAPTER 15
RANDOMIZED BLOCK AND REPEATED MEASURES DESIGNS: DEPENDENT SAMPLES ANALYSES OF VARIANCE

DETAILED TEXTBOOK OUTLINE

Chapter 15

KEY TERMS AND DEFINITIONS

between-block variance The variance of the means of blocks.

block A set of subjects matched on the basis of some preexperimental similarity.

blocking factor The basis on which subjects are matched.

counterbalance assignment Assignment of treatment levels to subjects in a way that controls for sequence effects.

dependent samples ANOVA The analysis performed on the data from an experiment setup as either an *RB-k* or *RM-k* design.

$F = (\bar{T}_j - \bar{T}_{j\cdot})^2 / (2MS_{error}/n)$ A simplified version of the *a priori* *F*-test used to make planned comparisons following the dependent samples ANOVA.

fixed-order assignment Order in which treatment levels are experienced as determined by the intrinsic characteristics of the independent variable.

Friedman-Ranks ANOVA A nonparametric analogue of the parametric dependent samples ANOVA that is used to test for differences among two or more treatment groups.

F-R The symbol for the statistic computed in the Friedman-Ranks ANOVA.

$F\text{-}R = \{12/[nk(k + 1)]\}\Sigma(R^2_j) - 3n(k + 1)$ Formula for the statistic computed in the Friedman-Ranks ANOVA.

randomized block design An experimental design employing two or more levels of a single independent variable and a blocking factor.

RB-k Symbol for a randomized block design.

repeated measures design An experimental design employing two or more levels of a single independent variable in which each subject or sample element experiences all of the treatment levels.

RM-k Symbol for a repeated measures design.

222

Chapter 15

$\Sigma S^2/k$ Computational monomial used to compute the sums of squares associated with blocks or subjects in *RB-k* and *RM-k* designs.

within-block variance Variance of the scores within a block.

MASTERING THE LANGUAGE OF STATISTICS

Fill-in-the-Blanks

Write the appropriate term(s) in the space(s) provided.

In this chapter the focus is on analyses of variance that are used with dependent samples. One way to achieve dependency in sampling is by matching subjects on the basis of some pre-experimental similarity. When subjects are matched, the set of matched subjects is called a _____. The basis on which the subjects are matched, such as a mutual category, similar heredity, or premeasurement of the dependent variable, is called a _____ _____. Experimental designs that employ a single independent variable and a blocking factor are referred to as _____ _____ designs. This class of designs is symbolized ____-___. The term _____ indicates that each of the subjects within a block is randomly assigned to a different one of the *k* treatment levels.

Another way to achieve dependency in sampling is to employ a single independent variable and assign each subject or sample member to *all* treatment levels. This class of designs is called _____ _____ designs and is symbolized ____-___. The order in which the subjects experience the treatment levels is generally randomly assigned or assigned in such a way as to control for sequence effects. This latter type of assignment is called _____ assignment. At times, however, it is impossible to counterbalance or randomly assign treatment levels due to the intrinsic characteristics of the independent variable. In these cases, the technique used is a _____-_____ _____, an ordering in which the subjects experience the treatment levels as determined by the intrinsic characteristics of the independent variable.

In the analysis of *RB-k* and *RM-k* designs, the total source of variance is partitioned into component sources. In the analysis of an *RB-k* design, the total variation is partitioned into the variance of the means of blocks, called the _____-_____ _____ and the variance of the scores within a block, called the _____-_____ _____. In the analysis of an *RM-k* design the total variation is partitioned into _____-_____ and _____-_____ sources. In computing the variation attributable to block or subjects the monomial used is _____, where _____ represents the sum of the *k* measures on any given block in the *RB-k* design or on any given subject in the *RM-k* design.

As with other experimental designs, a significant *F*-value obtained in ANOVA on *RB-k* and *RM-k* designs, when $k > 2$, directs you to analyze the data further. The *F*-test for making planned comparisons following the dependent samples ANOVA is given by the formula: _____.

A frequently used nonparametric analogue of the parametric dependent samples ANOVA is the _____-_____ ANOVA.

Chapter 15

The test statistic for this ANOVA is _____. The test statistic
is obtained by the following formula:

_____.

True-False Items

*Place a T for true or an F for false in the space provided
before each item.*

1. ____ A dependent samples ANOVA is used with *RB-k* and *CR-k*
designs.

2. ____ When subjects are matched on the basis of some pre-
experimental similarity, a set of subjects is referred
to as a block.

3. ____ The basis on which subjects are matched, such as a
mutual category, is called a matching factor.

4. ____ Experimental designs that employ a single independent
variable and a blocking factor are called repeated
measures designs.

5. ____ The symbol for an experimental design employing a single
independent variable and a blocking factor is *RB-k,*
where *k* represents the number of subjects in the
experiment.

6. ____ Experimental designs that employ a single independent
variable and assign each subject or sample member to
only one level of the independent variable are called
repeated measures designs.

7. ____ The term repeated measures refers to the procedure of
obtaining a measure of the dependent variable for each
subject or sample member for each of the *k*-treatment
levels.

8. ____ Assigning treatment levels to subjects in a way that
controls for sequence effects is called counterbalance
assignment.

9. ____ An ordering in which the subject experiences the
treatment levels as determined by the intrinsic
characteristics of the independent variable is called
fixed-order assignment.

10. ____ The analysis performed on the data from an experiment
set up as either an *RB-k* or *RM-k* design is called a
repeated measures ANOVA.

11.____ In the analysis of an *RB-k* design, the total variation is partitioned into between-subject and within-subject sources.

12.____ The Friedman-Ranks ANOVA is the nonparametric analogue of the parametric dependent samples ANOVA.

Multiple-Choice Items

Blacken out the letter corresponding to the correct answer.

1. Which of the following would not be involved in an *RB-k* design?
   (a) premeasuring subjects on the characteristic of interest
   (b) fixed-order assignment
   (c) matching subjects on a genetic basis
   (d) forming blocks on the basis of a mutual category

2. In an *RB-k* design, block refers to
   (a) a level of the independent variable.
   (b) a collection of dependent measures.
   (c) a set of matched subjects.
   (d) the characteristic of interest.

3. In the symbolization for a repeated measures design (*RM-k*), *k* refers to
   (a) the number of subjects per treatment level.
   (b) the number of measures per treatment level.
   (c) the number of treatment levels.
   (d) all of the above.

4. Assigning treatment levels to subjects in a way that controls for sequence effects is called
   (a) fixed-order assignment.
   (b) random assignment.
   (c) repeated measures assignment.
   (d) counterbalance assignment.

5. In an *RM-k* design, the within source of variation is partitioned into sources of variance attributable to
   (a) between- and within-blocks.
   (b) between- and within-subjects.
   (c) individual differences and experimental error.
   (d) treatment and experimental error.

6. In an *RB-k* design, the total variation is partitioned into the variance of the means called
   (a) between-block variance.
   (b) within-block variance.
   (c) variance due to experimental error.
   (d) variance due to treatment effects.

7. In an *RM-k* design, the total variation is partitioned into
   (a) between-block and within-block sources of variation.
   (b) between-subject and within-subject sources of variation.
   (c) variance attributable to treatment and experimental error.
   (d) between-group and within-group sources of variation.

8. The computation monomial used with *RB-k* and *RM-k* designs that is not used with *CR-k* designs is:
   (a) $\Sigma T_j^2/n$.
   (b) G^2/nk.
   (c) $\Sigma S^2/k$.
   (d) ΣX^2.

9. *F-R* is the symbol for a
   (a) nonparametric ANOVA test statistic.
   (b) parametric ANOVA test statistic.
   (c) test statistic for testing for heterogeneity of variance.
   (d) test statistic for making planned comparisons.

10. $F = (\bar{T}_j - \bar{T}_{j'})^2/(2MS_{error}/n)$ is the formula for
   (a) the Friedman-Ranks test statistic.
   (b) obtaining *F* in the dependent samples ANOVA.
   (c) planned comparisons following the parametric dependent samples ANOVA.
   (d) planned comparisons following the nonparametric dependent samples ANOVA.

11. Which monomial is not used in obtaining SS_{error} in the analysis of an *RM-k* design?
   (a) $\Sigma T_j^2/n$
   (b) $\Sigma S^2/n$
   (c) G^2/nk
   (d) ΣX^2

12. In the analysis of an *RM-k* design, $n(k - 1)$ is the formula for
   (a) $df_{between-subjects}$.
   (b) $df_{within-subjects}$.
   (c) $df_{treatment}$.
   (d) df_{error}.

APPLYING STATISTICAL CONCEPTS

Example Application

A behavioral scientist interested in four different types of therapy on obesity measures the weight of a large number of obese persons. Able to match five sets of 4 subjects on weight, age, and gender, the scientist randomly assigns to the members of each set a different therapy. The number of pounds lost under each therapy is given in Table 15.1.

Table 15.1
The Number of Pounds (X) Lost by Five Sets of Individuals Matched on Weight, Age, and Gender with Each Member of a Set Randomly Assigned a Different One of Four Therapeutic Programs (N per Therapeutic Program = 5). The Values for X^2 and Summary Measures, S, T, and G, Are Included to Facilitate Analysis.

Block	Therapy$_1$		Therapy$_2$		Therapy$_3$		Therapy$_4$			
	X	X^2	X	X^2	X	X^2	X	X^2	S	S^2
1	20	400	15	225	13	169	11	121	59	3481
2	25	625	16	256	12	144	15	225	68	4624
3	22	484	20	400	11	121	14	196	67	4489
4	21	441	15	225	14	196	10	100	60	3600
5	23	529	16	256	16	256	11	121	66	4356

$\Sigma S^2 =$ 20550

$T_j = 111 \qquad 82 \qquad 66 \qquad 61 \qquad G = 320$

$T_j^2/5 = 2464.2 \quad 1344.8 \quad 871.2 \quad 744.2 \quad \Sigma(T_j^2/5) = 5424.4$

$$\Sigma X^2 = 5490$$

In this example, sets of matched subjects called **blocks** are formed by matching the subjects on the basis of several *mutual categories*, weight, age, and gender, that have the potential to have a distinct influence on the dependent variable, weight loss. The different sets of subjects constitute a **blocking factor**. The experimental design employing a single independent variable such as type of therapy and a blocking factor is called a **randomized block design**. The term *randomized* indicates that the treatment levels (in this example therapies 1, 2, 3, and 4) are randomly assigned to subjects within a block. Assuming normality and homogeneity of variance of the dependent measure in the treatment populations, the analysis performed on the data from an experiment set up as an **RB-k** design is the parametric **dependent samples ANOVA**. Performing the dependent samples ANOVA requires obtaining values for four computational monomials, symbolized: $(1) = G^2/nk$, $(2) = \Sigma X^2$, $(3) = \Sigma T_j^2/n$, and $(4) = \Sigma S^2/k$. In this example, $(1) = 5120$, $(2) = 5490$, $(3) = 5424.4$, and $(4) = 5137.5$. Once the computational values are obtained, the sums of squares are obtained by the following formulas: $SS_{between\ blocks} = (4) - (1)$, $SS_{within\ blocks} = (2) - (4)$, $SS_{therapy} = (3) - (1)$, $SS_{error} = (2) - (4) - (3) + (1)$, and $SS_{total} = (2) - (1)$. Application of these formulas to this example yields the values in Table 15.2.

Table 15.2
ANOVA Summary Table for the Hypothetical Obesity Experiment

Computational Symbol Values	Source of Variation	*SS*	*df*	*MS*	*F*
(*1*) = 5120	Between Blocks	17.5	4	4.4	
(*2*) = 5490	Within Blocks	352.5	15	23.5	
(*3*) = 5424.4	Therapy	304.4	3	101.5	25.4
(*4*) = 5137.5	Error	48.1	12	4.0	
	Total	370.0	19		

The values for *df* in Table 15.2 are calculated by the following formulas: $df_{\text{between blocks}} = n - 1$, $df_{\text{within blocks}} = n(k - 1)$, $df_{\text{therapy}} = k - 1$, $df_{\text{error}} = (n - 1)(k - 1)$, and $df_{\text{total}} = nk - 1$. The *MS*'s are obtained by dividing the *SS* by its corresponding *df* and the *F* is the ratio of MS_{therapy} to MS_{error}.

The decision rule for evaluating H_0: $\mu_1 = \mu_2 = \mu_3 = \mu_4$ is: If $F_{\text{calc}} \geq F_{\text{table}}$, then reject H_0. In our example, since $F_{\text{calc}} = 25.4$ and $F_{\text{table}} = 3.49$ for 3 and 12 degrees of freedom at the 5% level of significance, H_0 is rejected. Stated formally, the results of the experiment indicate that the different therapies have different effects on weight loss, $F(3,12) = 25.4$, $p < 0.05$.

If the scientist had planned to make specific comparisons during the planning stage of the experiment, the *a priori F*-test could have been used to compare treatment means. For example,

$$F_{\text{therapy 1 vs therapy 2}} =$$

$$(\bar{T}_{\text{therapy 1}} - \bar{T}_{\text{therapy 2}})^2/(2MS_{\text{error}}/n) =$$

$$(22.2 - 16.4)^2/[2(25.4)/5] = 3.31.$$

The F_{table} for 1 and 12 *df* with $\alpha = 0.05$ is 4.75; H_0: $\mu_{\text{therapy 1}} = \mu_{\text{therapy 2}}$, therefore, is not rejected. The nonparametric analogue of the parametric dependent samples ANOVA, the **Friedman-Ranks ANOVA**, can also be appropriately applied to the data in this example because the samples are random dependent samples, two conditions required by the Friedman-Ranks ANOVA. The Friedman-Ranks ANOVA, however, also requires that measures taken on the dependent variable within each block be ranked independently. The smallest score for each block is assigned the lowest rank, the next smallest score is given the next lowest rank and so on. These ranks for the data in Table 15.1 are given in Table 15.3.

Table 15.3
The Ranks within Blocks for the Data of Table 15.1

Block	Therapy$_1$	Therapy$_2$	Therapy$_3$	Therapy$_4$
1	4	3	2	1
2	4	3	1	2
3	4	3	1	2
4	4	3	2	1
5	4	2.5	2.5	1
$R_j=$	20	14.5	8.5	7

The test statistic **F-R** for the Friedman-Ranks ANOVA is calculated by the formula: $\{12/[nk(k + 1)]\}\Sigma(R_j) - 3n(k + 1)$, where R_i is the sum of the ranks for a given treatment level. In our example, $K\text{-}W = \{12/[20(4 + 1)]\}[20^2 + 14.5^2 + 8.5^2 + 7^2] - 3(5)(4 + 1) = 12.8$. The decision rule for the Friedman-Ranks ANOVA is: If $F\text{-}R_{calc} \geq F_{table}$, reject H_0. The calculated value of $F\text{-}R$ (12.8) for the hypothetical obesity experiment is larger than the critical value (7.81) in Appendix Table 10 in the textbook with $df = 3$ and $\alpha = 0.05$. You conclude, therefore, that type of therapy is a statistically significant factor in the weight loss of obese subjects, $F\text{-}R(3) = 12.8$, $p < 0.05$.

Application Exercises

1. Memory retrieval is enhanced if the learned material is organized in some way during the encoding process. Various strategies, called mnemonic devices, have been used to organize lists of material to be learned so as to facilitate retrieval. One such strategy, called narrative chaining, requires the learner to relate the materials in the list in story fashion. A second strategy, called the peg word method, has the learner form images of the materials to be learned in an interactive fashion with a previously learned list of words called pegs. A third strategy, called the method of loci, has the learner mentally place information to be retrieved at various locations in an imagined familiar setting. Believing that some methods are more effective than others, a psychology instructor randomly selects nine students from a large psychology class to participate in an experiment involving the three mentioned mnemonic devices. Three different 30 item lists of equal difficulty are formed and each student is asked to learn each list using a different one of the mnemonic devices during the learning process. The order and method by which each list was learned differed from student to student. One student, for example, learns List A by the method of loci, List B by the peg word method, and List C by the narrative chaining procedure in that order. Another subject learns List C by

the peg word method, List A by the narrative chaining procedure, and List B by the method of loci in that order, and so on. Twenty four hours after the lists are learned to one perfect recitation, the students are asked to recall as many of the items in each list as possible. Table 15.4 presents the data from this hypothetical experiment.

Table 15.4
The Number of Items Recalled 24 Hours after Learning Each of Three Lists of 30 Items Each Using A Different Memory Strategy (Narrative, Peg Word, Loci) for Each List ($N = 9$). Extra Workspace is Provided for Calculations.

Student	Narrative	Peg Word	Loci
1	25	18	20
2	27	25	18
3	18	17	19
4	26	27	25
5	19	18	17
6	16	17	18
7	20	19	16
8	22	18	20
9	17	16	15

Assuming the data meet the conditions for performing a parametric dependent samples ANOVA, specify

a. the type of design substituting a numerical value for k.

b. the procedure (matching or repeating measures) by which dependency in sampling is achieved.

c. the basis on which samples are matched for an *RB-k* design or the type of assignment for an *RM-k* design.

d. an appropriate nondirectional research hypothesis.

e. the null and alternative hypotheses in words.

f. the null hypothesis in symbols.

g. the general decision rule.

h. a specific decision rule for $\alpha = 0.05$ and the appropriate *df*.

2. a. Perform the necessary calculations on the data in Table 15.4 to determine values for G, ΣX^2, $\Sigma T_j^2/n$, ΣS^2. (Show work in Table 15.4.)

b. Obtain values for computational symbols (*1*), (*2*), (*3*) and (*4*).

c. Summarize the ANOVA results in Table 15.5.
Table 15.5
Summary Table for ANOVA Performed on the Data from Table 15.4

Computational Symbol Values	Source of Variation	*SS*	*df*	*MS*	*F*
(*1*) = _____	Betw._____	_____	_____	_____	
(*2*) = _____	Within_____	_____	_____	_____	
(*3*) = _____	Strategy	_____	_____	_____	
(*4*) = _____	Error	_____	_____	_____	_____
	Total	_____	_____		

3. On the basis of the analysis performed for part *2,*

   a. reach a decision about H_0.

   b. reach a conclusion about the research hypothesis as you would in a formal research report.

   c. further analyze the data using the *a priori F*-test, if appropriate.

4. An animal behaviorist believes that level of illumination is an important factor in the maze performance of albino rats. A large number of rats are randomly selected from the university animal colony and are given five trials in a complex maze in which a sucrose solution is to be found in the goal box. The number of incorrect alleys entered on the way to the goal box is recorded for each rat. The investigator is able to form six sets of rats so that the number of blind alley entries was the same for the rats in a set but differed from set to set. The animals from each set are randomly placed in a different illumination level group and are given five additional trials in the maze. The number of incorrect alleys entered on the way to the goal box is again recorded for the five trials. The data are shown in Table 15.6

Table 15.6
The Number of Incorrect Alleys Entered by Rats Run Under
Different Illumination Levels in a Complex Maze during a
Second Set of Five Training Trials (N = 24)

Level$_1$	Rank$_1$	Level$_2$	Rank$_2$	Level$_3$	Rank$_3$	Level$_4$	Rank$_4$
15		17		18		13	
14		16		15		16	
16		18		19		15	
14		15		16		13	
17		18		20		19	
20		22		21		19	

*Assuming that the data in Table 15.6 do not meet the
conditions necessary to perform the parametric dependent
samples ANOVA, determine*

a. the type of design substituting a numerical value for *k*.

b. the procedure (matching or repeating measures) by which
dependency in sampling is achieved.

c. the basis on which samples are matched for an *RB-k*
design or the type of assignment for an *RM-k* design.

d. an appropriate nondirectional research hypothesis.

e. the null and alternative hypotheses in words.

f. the test statistic.

g. the general decision rule.

h. a specific decision rule for $\alpha = 0.05$ and the appropriate *df*.

i. a value for the test statistic. Determine R_j's in Table 15.6.

j. whether H_0 should or should not be rejected.

k. what your decision about H_0 means in terms of the research hypothesis.

l. how you would report your results in a formal research report.

MEETING THE CHALLENGE OF STATISTICS

The following problems pertain to the memory experiment described in the *Meeting the Challenge of Statistics* section in Chapter 1, pages 9-10, of this workbook. The data from the control group presented emotionally laden words are presented in Table 15.7. Assume that these data constitute a separate experiment and that the experimenter believes that there will be a difference in the numbers of pleasant and unpleasant words recalled.

Table 15.7
Data and Workspace Necessary to Complete ANOVA for The Following
Problems

Subject		1	2	3	4	5	6	7	8	9	10	T	T_j^2/n
Pleas.	X	7	9	6	7	8	7	6	9	6	5		
	X^2												
Unpleas.	X	5	5	5	6	7	7	7	4	5	7		
	X^2												
	S												
	S^2												

1. Specify the type of design substituting a numerical value for k.

2. Name the procedure (matching or repeating measures) by which dependency in sampling is achieved.

3. Indicate the basis on which samples are matched for an $RB-k$ design or the type of assignment for an $RM-k$ design.

4. State an appropriate nondirectional research hypothesis.

5. Symbolize the null and alternative hypotheses for the parametric dependent samples ANOVA.

6. Obtain values for G, ΣX^2, $\Sigma T_j^2/n$, ΣS^2. (Show work in Table 15.8.)

7. Obtain values for the computational symbols (*1*), (*2*), (*3*), and (*4*).

8. Put the results of your ANOVA in a summary Table.

9. Give the specific decision rule for $\alpha = 0.05$ and the appropriate *df*.

10. Reach a conclusion about H_0.

11. State what your decision about H_0 means in terms of the research hypothesis.

12. Report the outcome of the experiment as you would in a formal research report.

CHAPTER 16
COMPLETELY RANDOMIZED FACTORIAL
DESIGNS AND THE TWO-WAY ANALYSIS OF VARIANCE

DETAILED TEXTBOOK OUTLINE

Chapter 16

Answers to Progress Assessments (Page 389)

KEY TERMS AND DEFINITIONS

A, B Symbols in a two-way ANOVA that are used to represent independent variables of a completely randomized factorial design.

A_1, A_2, B_1, B_2 Symbols used to designate sums of treatment levels a_1, a_2, b_1, b_2, respectively.

a_1, a_2, ... a_p, b_1, b_2, ... b_q Symbols used to designate treatment levels of factors A, B.

AB Symbol used to refer to the combined treatments A and B and also to the interaction of the two variables.

additive interaction When one variable has the same effect across levels of the other variable.

completely randomized factorial design An experimental design involving two or more levels of each of two or more independent variables.

CRF-pq Symbols for a completely randomized factorial design where p and q refer to the number of treatment levels of the two independent variables.

$CV = \sqrt{F_{table}[MS_{wg}(1/np + 1/np)]}$ The formula for a critical value for mean differences of a B-variable.

eta-squared (η^2) A biased estimate of the extent to which a dependent variable is influenced by an independent variable. It is the ratio of SS for any given treatment or interaction of treatments to SS_{tot} expressed as a percentage.

$$F_A \text{ at } b_j = \frac{\{[(AB_{1j})^2 + (AB_{2j})^2 + ... + (AB_{pj})^2]/n - (B_j^2/np)\}/(p-1)}{MS_{wg}}$$

General expression for testing the simple main effect of A at b_j in a two-factor experiment.

factorial experiment An experiment in which each treatment level of any one independent variable is administered in conjunction with each and every treatment level of the other variables.

$F = (\overline{AB}_{1j} - \overline{AB}_{1'j})^2 / [MS_{wg}(1/n + 1/n)]$ Formula for testing the simple main effect of A at b_j when there are two levels of A in a *CRF-pq* design.

$F = (\overline{AB}_{1j} - \overline{AB}_{1j'})^2 / [MS_{wg}(1/n + 1/n)]$ Formula for testing the simple main effect of B at a_i when there are two levels of B in a *CRF-pq* design.

$F = (\overline{A}_i - \overline{A}_{i'})^2 / [MS_{wg}(1/nq + 1/nq)]$ Formula for comparing means for the main effect of A-variable in a *CRF-pq* design.

$F = (MS_A$ at $b_2)/MS_{wg}$ Formula for testing the simple main effect of A at b_2.

fixed factors   Variables whose treatment levels have been selected on some predetermined nonrandom basis.

interaction effects   The effects on the dependent variable of one independent variable across levels of another independent variable.

main effects   The effects of levels of individual independent variables on the dependent variable.

nonadditive interaction   When one variable has a different effect across levels of another variable.

p, q   Letters used to designate the number of treatment levels of variables A and B, respectively.

random factors   Variables whose treatment levels have been selected randomly.

simple main effects   The effects of all levels of one variable at each level of another variable.

SS_A at $b_2 = \{[(AB_{12})^2 + (AB_{22})^2]/n\} - (B_2^2/np)$ The sum of squares for variable A at level b_2 in a factorial experiment with only two levels of A.

two-way ANOVA   The analysis used to evaluate the data from an experiment involving two independent variables and a single dependent measure taken on each sample member (*CRF-pq* design).

Chapter 16

MASTERING THE LANGUAGE OF STATISTICS

Fill-in-the-Blanks

Write the appropriate term(s) in the space(s) provided.

If each treatment level of one independent variable is administered in conjunction with each and every treatment level of other independent variables, and only one dependent measure is recorded for each subject in the experiment, the experiment is referred to as a _____ experiment and the experimental design is called a _____

_____ factorial design. If the experimental design involves only two independent variables, the design of the experiment is symbolized ____-____, where p refers to the number of levels of the independent variable designed ____ and q refers to the number of levels of the independent variable designated _____. The individual levels of the A-variable are designated ____,___, ... _____, and the individual levels of the B-variable are designated ____, _____, ... _____. The symbol ____ also represents the sum of all the scores under a specified level of the A-variable. For example, _____ symbolizes the sum of all the scores under treatment level a_1. Similarly, the symbol _____ represents the sum of all the scores under treatment level b_2. These sums are needed to compute the _____effects of the A- and B-variables, respectively. The main effects in a *CRF-pq* experimental design are evaluated by a _____-_____ _____. The two-way ANOVA is used to evaluate not only _____ _____, which are the effects of the levels of the individual independent variables on the dependent variable, but also to evaluate _____ effects, which are the effects on the dependent variable of one variable across levels of the other variable. The symbol AB refers to the _____ of the variables A and B.

The interpretation of the two-way ANOVA depends, in part, on whether the variables or factors in the experiment are _____ factors, factors selected on some predetermined nonrandom basis, or _____ factors, factors for which the treatment levels are selected randomly. If the factors are _____ factors, then all treatment levels about which conclusions can be drawn are included in the experiment. With _____ factors, however, the ANOVA is simplified because the denominator of all F-ratios is the within-group mean square. The interpretation of the two-way ANOVA also depends, in part, on whether or not the _____ effect is significant. For example, if there are only two levels of the B-variable and the main effect of B is significant, but the _____ of A and B is not, then simply by looking at the means of the B-levels, you could conclude that one level of B is more or less effective than the other level. In such a case the interaction effect is called an _____ interaction. If, on the other hand, there is a significant _____ effect, then B may not be having the same effect across all levels of A and the effect of the B-variable cannot be simply interpreted. If such is the case, the interaction effect is

242

referred to as a _____ interaction. If the
interaction is nonadditive, the _____ _____ effects
may need to be assessed. _____ _____ effects are the
effects of all levels of one variable at each level of another
variable. The test for the simple main effect of B at a_i when
there are only two levels of the B-variable is given by the
formula: _____.
Similarly, a test of the simple main effect of A at b_j is
given by the formula: _____.
When there are more than two levels of the independent
variable, a test for _____ _____effects requires
calculating SS and MS for the effect of one variable at each
level of the other variable and computing F in the usual
manner by dividing the calculated MS by the MS_{wg}. For
example, for assessing the effect of A at b_2, $F =$
_____. The general expression for testing the
simple main effect of A at b_j is given in the following
formula: _____

_____. When the
ANOVA yields significant main or interaction effects,
_____ refers to the difference between the observed
treatment mean and the mean of the sampling distribution. The
term _____ means this difference is larger than would
be expected by chance. The term _____ does not
indicate that the effect is meaningful or the extent to which
the dependent variable is influenced by an independent
variable. You can, however, estimate the extent to which a

dependent variable is influenced by an independent variable by

calculating a value called _____-_____, symbolized _____.

_____-_____ is the ratio of the sum of squares for any

given variable or interaction of variables to the total sum of

squares expressed as a percentage.

True-False Items

*Place a T for true or an F for false in the space provided
before each item.*

1. ____ The effects of the levels of individual independent
variables on the dependent variable are called main
effects.

2. ____ The effects on the dependent variable of one variable
across levels of the other variable are called cross-
over effects.

3. ____ The symbol *AB* refers to the combined treatments *A* and
B and to the interaction of the variables *A* and *B*.

4. ____ Factors selected on some predetermined nonrandom basis
are called fixed factors.

5. ____ The effects of all levels of one variable at each
level of another variable are called simple main
effects.

6. ____ When one variable has a different effect across levels
of the other variable, there is said to be an additive
interaction.

7. ____ Nonadditive interaction effects are significant.

8. ____ The letters used to designate the number of levels of
the *A* and *B* variables, respectively, are *a* and *b*.

9. ____ The extent to which a dependent variable is influenced
by an independent variable is symbolized by r^2.

10. ____ The symbol for a completely randomized design is *CRF-
pq*, where *p* and *q* refer to the number of independent
and dependent variables, respectively.

11. ____ A completely randomized factorial design is an
experimental design in which the levels of the
independent variables have been selected randomly.

12.____ Fixed factors simplify the two-way ANOVA but limit the generality of the results.

Multiple-Choice Items

Blacken out the letter corresponding to the correct answer.

1. Unlike the _____ANOVA, the _____ANOVA is easily applicable to experiments in which there are not equal numbers of sample members under each treatment level.
   (a) one-way, two-way
   (b) two-way, one-way
   (c) dependent samples, independent samples
   (d) independent samples, dependent samples

2. The effects on the dependent variable of one variable across levels of the other variable are called _____ effects.
   (a) main
   (b) interaction
   (c) simple main
   (d) significant

3. The individual levels of variable *A* are designated
   (a) $p_1, p_2, \cdots p_q$.
   (b) $A_1, A_2, \cdots A_p$.
   (c) $a_1, a_2, \cdots a_p$.
   (d) $q_1, q_2, \cdots q_p$.

4. The symbol AB_{ij} refers to
   (a) the combined treatments *A* and *B*.
   (b) the interaction of treatments *A* and *B*.
   (c) the sum of the scores of sample members given treatment levels A_i and B_j.
   (d) the sum of the scores of sample members given treatment levels a_i and b_j.

5. The df_{bg} in a two-way ANOVA equals
   (a) $npq - 1$.
   (b) $pq(n - 1)$.
   (c) $pq - 1$.
   (d) $(p - 1)(q - 1)$.

6. Factors selected on some predetermined nonrandom basis are called
   (a) fixed factors.
   (b) predetermined factors.
   (c) randomized factors.
   (d) none of the above.

7. The effects of all levels of one variable at each level of another variable are called
   (a) interaction effects.

Chapter 16

(b) cross-over effects.
(c) simple main effects.
(d) interaction effects.

8. The symbol η^2
   (a) refers to a parameter.
   (b) is the coefficient of determination.
   (c) refers to a biased statistic.
   (d) refers to an unbiased statistic.

9. Eta-squared
   (a) is symbolized η^2.
   (b) estimates the percentage of variability in the dependent variable that can be attributed to an independent variable.
   (c) is the ratio of the sum of squares for any given treatment or interaction of treatments to the total sum of squares expressed as a percentage.
   (d) all of the above.

10. When one variable has the same effect across levels of another variable there is said to be
    (a) a significant interaction.
    (b) an additive interaction.
    (c) a nonadditive interaction.
    (d) a significant main effect.

11. The df_{wg} equals
    (a) $npq - 1$.
    (b) $pq(n - 1)$.
    (c) $pq - 1$.
    (d) $(p - 1)(q - 1)$.

12. The formula $F = (MS_A$ at $b_2)/MS_{wg}$ is used to test
    (a) the main effect of A at b_2.
    (b) the interaction effect of A at b_2.
    (c) simple main effect of A at b_2.
    (d) the main effect of b_2 at A.

APPLYING STATISTICAL CONCEPTS

Example Application

A researcher wishes to determine the effects of 6, 12, and 18 hours of water deprivation on the random activity of young and adult rats. After the appropriate deprivation period, the rats are individually placed in a small rectangular cage and the number of times each rat crosses from one side of the cage to the other in a 20-minute period is counted. These counts are used as a measure of random activity.
    You may recognize that the design of this experiment is a

completely randomized factorial design (*CRF*-23), where the 2 refers to the levels of the **A-variable**, age, and 3 refers to the levels of the **B-variable**, hours of water deprivation. You may also realize that the variable or factors are **fixed factors**, factors selected on some predetermined nonrandom basis. If you assume that the samples are random independent samples, that the counts are normally distributed in the populations from which the samples are selected, and that there is homogeneity of variance, then you should agree that the **two-way ANOVA** would be used to analyze the data collected in this experiment. The data and the application of the two-way ANOVA is illustrated in the accompanying table.

Table 16.1
The Hypothetical Number of Cage Crossings Made by Young and Adult Rats after Periods of 6, 12, and 18 Hours of Water Deprivation and Computational Procedures (i), Computational Symbols and Values (ii), *SS* Formulas and Procedures (iii), *df* Formulas and Computations (iv), and the Two-Factor ANOVA Summary Table (v)

(i)

Young Rats				Adult Rats		

Level of Deprivation (Hours)

ab_{11}	ab_{12}	ab_{13}		ab_{21}	ab_{22}	ab_{23}
<u>6</u>	<u>12</u>	<u>18</u>		<u>6</u>	<u>12</u>	<u>18</u>
2	6	10		5	5	15
4	8	12		6	7	12
3	6	11		7	4	14
4	9	13		8	9	13
2	6	<u>14</u>		4	5	<u>11</u>

$AB_{11} = 15$ $\qquad\qquad$ $AB_{21} = 30$
$\qquad AB_{12} = 35$ $\qquad\qquad\qquad$ $AB_{22} = 30$
$\qquad\qquad AB_{13} = 60$ $\qquad\qquad\qquad\qquad$ $AB_{23} = 65$

$A_1 = 15 + 35 + 60 = 110 \qquad A_2 = 30 + 30 + 65 = 125$
$B_1 = 15 + 30 = 45 \quad B_2 = 35 + 30 = 65 \quad B_3 = 60 + 65 = 125$
$G = 110 + 125 = 235$

(ii)
$(1) = G^2/npq = 235^2/5(2)(3) = 1840.83$
$(2) = \Sigma X^2 = 2^2 + 4^2 + \ldots + 13^2 + 11^2 = 2273$
$(3) = \Sigma A^2/nq = (110^2 + 125^2)/5(3) = 1848.33$
$(4) = \Sigma B^2/np = (45^2 + 65^2 + 125^2)/5(2) = 2187.5$
$(5) = \Sigma(AB)^2/n = (15^2 + 35^2 + 60^2 + 30^2 + 30^2 + 65^2)/5 = 2215.0$

(iii)

$SS_{bg} = (5) - (1) = 2215.00 - 1840.83 = 374.17$
$SS_A = (3) - (1) = 1848.33 - 1840.83 = 7.50$
$SS_B = (4) - (1) = 2187.50 - 1840.83 = 346.67$
$SS_{AB} = (5)-(4)-(3)+(1) = 2215.0-2187.5-1848.33+1840.83 = 20.00$
$SS_{wg} = (2) - (5) = 2273.00 - 2215.00 = 58.00$
$SS_{tot} = (2) - (1) = 2273.00 - 1840.83 = 432.17$

(iv)

$df_{bg} = pq - 1 = 6 - 1 = 5$
$df_A = p - 1 = 2 - 1 = 1$
$df_B = q - 1 = 3 - 1 = 2$
$df_{AB} = (p - 1)(q - 1) = (2 - 1)(3 - 1) = 2$
$df_{wg} = pq(n - 1) = 2(3)(5 - 1) = 24$
$df_{tot} = npq - 1 = 5(2)(3) - 1 = 29$

(v)

Source	SS	df	MS	F
Between-Groups	374.17	5	74.83	30.9
A (Age of rats)	7.50	1	7.50	3.1
B (Hours of Deprivation)	346.67	2	173.34	71.6
AB (Interaction)	20.00	2	10.00	4.1
Within-Groups	58.00	24	2.42	
Total	432.17	29		

The general decision rule for the two-way ANOVA is that if $F_{calc} \geq F_{table}$, then reject H_0. Since the calculated $F_{bg} = 30.9$ and $F_{table} = 2.62$ for 5 and 24 df at $\alpha = 0.05$, the between group H_0 is rejected. This not only indicates that there is a significant difference among groups but also indicates that further analysis is required. Further analysis indicates that the main effect of the A-variable, age of rats, is not significant, $F(1,24) = 3.1$, $p > 0.05$. Further analysis also indicates, however, that the main effect of the B-variable, hours of deprivation, and the interaction of the A-variable and B-variable is significant, $Fs(2,24) \geq 4.1$, $p < 0.05$. Since the interaction is **nonadditive**, a test for **simple main effects** is necessary for a correct interpretation of the two-way ANOVA. Since there are more than two levels of the B-variable, the test for simple main effects of B requires computing SS and MS for the effect of B at each level of the A-variable. The SS for the simple main effect of B (hours of deprivation) at a_1 (young rats) is as follows:

$$SS_B \text{ at } a_1 = [(AB_{11})^2 + (AB_{12})^2 + (AB_{13})^2]/n - A_1^2/nq$$
$$= [(15^2) + (35^2) + (60^2)]/5 - 110^2/(5)(3)$$
$$= 1010.0 - 806.7 = 203.3$$

The df for the simple main effect of B at a_1 is $q - 1 = 3 - 1 = 2$. The MS for the simple main effect of B at a_1, then, is:

$$MS_B \text{ at } a_1 = (SS_B \text{ at } a_1)/(q - 1) = 203.3/2 = 101.6$$

The F for B at a_1 is $(MS_B$ at $a_1)/MS_{wg} = 101.6/2.42 = 42.0$.

The results of this test indicate that there is a significant effect of *hours of deprivation* on young rats. There should be a similar test for the simple main effect of B at a_2 (adult rats). Also a test for the simple main effects of A across levels of B is also appropriate. Since there are only two levels of A, the F-test is simplified as follows:

$$F \text{ for } A \text{ at } b_2 = (\overline{AB}_{12} - \overline{AB}_{22})^2/[MS_{wg}(1/n+1/n)]$$
$$= [7 - 6]^2/[2.24(1/5 + 1/5)] = 1/0.97 = 1.0$$

This test indicates that there is no difference in activity between young and adult rats when rats are deprived of water for 12 hours, $F(1,24) = 1.0$, $p > 0.05$. Similar tests for the effect of age at 6 and 18 hours of deprivation can also be performed.

A significant main or interaction effect does not indicate that the effect is meaningful or the extent to which the independent variables influence the dependent variable. This, however, can be estimated by calculating η^2. This statistic is the ratio of the sum of squares for any given independent variable or interaction to the total sum of squares expressed as a percentage. In our example, SS_B (where B refers to hours of deprivation) equals 346.67 and SS_{tot} equals 432.17. Eta-squared, therefore, equals $346.67/342.17 = 0.80$. This means that the percentage of variability in the activity counts of the rats that is attributable to water deprivation level is approximately 80 (that is, 0.80 X 100).

Application Exercises

1. In an animal learning experiment four groups of eight rats each were given fifty training trials on a spatial discrimination in a T-shaped maze. In this apparatus, called a T-maze, the rat runs down the stem of the T to the cross arm where it must choose to go right or left. For all rats there are food pellets at the right end of the arm. There are no food pellets at the end of the left arm. The first variable manipulated is hours of food deprivation. Half the subjects are deprived of food for 6 hours and the other half are deprived 12 hours before training. The second variable manipulated is number of food pellets presented. One group of rats is deprived of food for 6 hours and is rewarded with two food pellets for making a right turn at the choice point. Another group of rats is food-deprived for 6 hours and is rewarded with one food pellet for making a right turn at the choice point. The remaining two groups are deprived of food for 12 hours. One of these groups is rewarded with one food pellet and the other with two food pellets for making a

right turn at the choice point. The dependent measure is the number of times out of fifty that the rat chooses the rewarded end of the cross arm. Hypothetical data for this experiment are shown in Table 16.2.

Table 16.2
The Number of Times Out of Fifty that Animals Deprived of Food for 6 or 12 Hours Choose the End of the Cross Arm of the Maze That Contains a Food Reward (One or Two Pellets)

	6 Hours Deprived		12 Hours Deprived		
	X	X^2	X	X^2	
	29		34		
	31		37		
One Pellet	27		33		
	30		32		
	32	____	33	____	
$AB =$					$B_1 =$ ____
$\Sigma X^2_{AB} =$					
$s^2_{AB} =$					
Two Pellets	35		39		
	37		37		
	32		41		
	33		42		
	36	____	40	____	
$AB =$					
$\Sigma X^2_{AB} =$					$B_2 =$ ____
$s^2_{AB} =$					
$A_1 =$ ____		$A_2 =$ ____		$G =$ ____	
		$\Sigma X^2 =$			

Assuming that the samples are randomized independent samples from normal populations,

a. fill in Table 16.2 and use the s^2 values to perform the test for heterogeneity of variance.

    b. name and assign letter symbols to the first and second independent variables.

    c. symbolize the experimental design assigning numbers to the letter designations of levels of the independent variables.

    d. symbolize the sum of the scores for each of the four treatment groups.

    e. symbolize the sum of the scores for all the animals deprived for 6 hours (and for 12 hours).

    f. symbolize the sum of the scores for all the animals rewarded with one pellet (and with 2 pellets).

    g. compute the values for the computational symbols (*1*), (*2*), (*3*), (*4*), and (*5*) from Table 16.2.

    h. compute values for all *SS*.

    i.   compute values for all *df*.

    j.   perform the two-way ANOVA putting the results in a summary table.

    k.   state if tests for simple main effects are necessary and explain the reasoning behind your answer.

    l.   state if tests for main effects are necessary and explain the reasoning behind your answer.

    m.   state the results as in a formal research report.

2. In another experiment on spatial discrimination learning by rats in a T-maze, the apparatus is modified by inserting chambers between the choice point and the ends of the cross arm of the maze. The purpose of the chambers is to delay the animals from reaching the end of the arm after a choice is made. By varying how long the rats are kept in the delay chamber, the experimenter can control the time between making a correct choice and receiving the food reward. Again the amount of reward (one versus two pellets) is varied, variable *B*. Also varied is the time the rats are kept in the delay chamber, variable *A*. The times are 1 second, 15 seconds, and 225 seconds. Again, the number of correct choices out of 50 training trials is the dependent measure. Hypothetical data from this experiment are given in Table 16.3.

Table 16.3
The Number of Times Out of Fifty That Rats Delayed for 1, 15, or 225 Seconds after Making a Correct Choice Chose the End of the Arm Containing a Food Reward (One or Two Food Pellets).

	Time in Delay Chamber		
	1 second	15 seconds	225 seconds
one pellet	35	25	15
	36	28	16
	39	27	20
	40	30	18
	41	31	21
two pellets	39	40	42
	40	36	39
	41	35	35
	34	37	40
	37	41	38

Assuming that the samples are randomized independent samples from normal populations with equal variances,

a. calculate appropriate sums in Table 16.3.

b. determine values for computational number symbols.

c. determine values for all *SS*.

d. determine values for *df*.

e. perform the two-way ANOVA putting the results in a summary table and an asterisk by the *F*-values that are significant.

f. test for the simple main effects of A (number of food pellets) at each level of B and indicate which are significant.

g. interpret the results of the two-way ANOVA and the tests for simple main effects as you would in a formal research report.

h. determine how much of the variability in correct choices is due to the number of food pellets.

i. determine how much of the variability in correct choices is due to the delay of reward.

j. determine how much of the variability in correct choices is due to the interaction of number of food pellets and delay of reward.

MEETING THE CHALLENGE OF STATISTICS

Chapter 16

The following problems pertain to the memory experiment described in the *Meeting the Challenge of Statistics* section in Chapter 1, pages 9-10, of this workbook. The data for that hypothetical experiment are given in Table 16.4.

Table 16.4
The Number of Correctly Recalled Syllables or Words by Freshman that Went to Sleep Immediately after Learning the List (Experimental) and by Freshman Who Remained Awake for at Least One Hour (Control)

| | Type of Item to Be Recalled | | |
	Nonsense Syllables	Neutral Words	Emotional Words
	12	12	15
	13	14	18
	11	13	16
	11	10	16
Experimental	9	14	13
	10	15	16
	13	11	16
	12	13	13
	12	16	15
	10	15	18
	10	10	12
	11	11	14
	9	12	11
	9	8	13
Control	6	9	15
	11	9	14
	6	9	13
	5	8	13
	8	11	11
	8	9	12

1. Letting the group (experimental, control) be the A-variable and the type of item to be recalled be the B-variable, symbolize and find the value of the individual AB-treatment groups.

Group	Symbol for Sum	Value of Sum
Nonsense/experimental	_____	_____
Nonsense/control	_____	_____
Neutral/experimental	_____	_____
Neutral/control	_____	_____
Emotion/experimental	_____	_____
Emotion/control	_____	_____

256

2. Symbolize the design of the experiment substituting numbers for the letter symbols for levels.

3. Symbolize and find the value of the sum of the experimental subjects, the control subjects, the subjects presented nonsense syllables, the subjects presented neutral words, and the subjects presented emotion laden words.

Subjects	Symbol for Sum	Value of Sum
Experimental		
Control		
Nonsense syllables		
Neutral words		
Emotion laden words		

4. Symbolize the monomials and find the values for the computations number symbols (1), (2), (3), (4), and (5).

Number Symbols	Monomial	Value
(1)		
(2)		
(3)		
(4)		
(5)		

5. Perform the two-way ANOVA on the data and put the results in the following summary table marking the significant F's with an asterisk.

Table 16.5
Summary Table for the Two-Way ANOVA Performed on the Data of Table 16.4.

Source	SS	df	MS	F
Between Groups				
A (Group)				
B (Item)				
AB (Interaction)				
Within Groups				
Total				

6. On the basis of the ANOVA, decide whether comparisons of means for main effects or tests of simple main effects need to be made.

7. Perform the tests necessary to correctly interpret the experimental results.

8. Put the results in reporting format.

CHAPTER 17
ANALYSIS OF FREQUENCY DATA OBTAINED FOR SPECIFIC CATEGORIES: CHI-SQUARE

DETAILED TEXTBOOK OUTLINE

Chapter 17

KEY TERMS AND DEFINITIONS

chi-square A statistic, symbolized χ^2, that is used to evaluate hypotheses when observations are classified into mutually exclusive categories and the frequency of observations in each category is determined.

$\chi^2 = \Sigma[(O - E)^2/E]$ Formula used to calculate χ^2 where O refers to the observed frequency of a particular category and E refers to the expected (or theoretical) frequency of a particular category.

χ^2-goodness-of-fit-test A statistical test used to evaluate hypotheses that sampled category proportions of a population are equal to hypothesized population proportions. The hypothesized population proportions are described in the null hypothesis.

χ^2 test of independence A test performed on frequency data to determine whether the way observations are categorized on the basis of one variable influences the way they are categorized on the basis of a second variable.

expected frequencies (E) The number of observations that should be obtained for a defined category based on statements given in the null hypothesis for tests involving χ^2.

$k - 1$ Formula used to determine df for χ^2-goodness-of-fit test involving hypothesized expected frequencies for one variable where k refers to the number of categories.

$k - 3$ Formula used to determine adjusted df for the χ^2-goodness-of-fit test of normality of a distribution where k equals the number of categories (class intervals) in the grouped frequency distribution.

observed frequencies (O) The actual observations for a defined category made by an investigator.

prop Symbol for proportions given in χ^2 statistical hypotheses.

$(r - 1)(c - 1)$ Formula used to determine df for the χ^2 test of independence when frequencies are in table format where r refers to the number of categories of one variable (number of rows in table) and c refers to the number of categories of the other variable (number of columns).

MASTERING THE LANGUAGE OF STATISTICS

Fill-in-the-Blanks

Chapter 17

Write the appropriate term(s) in the spaces(s) provided.

The statistic, _____-_____, symbolized _____, is used to evaluate statistical hypotheses when frequency data are collected for different categories. Computing chi-square requires an understanding of the terms, _____ _____, which refer to the number of observations that should be obtained on the basis of statements given in H_0, and the terms _____ _____, which refer to the actual observations made by an investigator. Expected frequencies are symbolized _____ and observed frequencies are symbolized _____. Given an understanding of these terms and symbols, a value for _____ can be obtained by the following formula:

$$\chi^2 = \sum \frac{(O - E)^2}{E}$$

When this formula is used to test whether sampled category proportions of a population are equal to hypothesized population proportions, the test is called the ____-_____-___-_____. Most often the alternative hypothesis for the _____ test is expressed as follows: observed frequencies will not equal expected frequencies. The null hypothesis is then _____. Frequently these hypotheses are more formally stated in relation to the expected frequencies expressed as proportions, symbolized _____. In most tests of goodness-of-fit, the *df* for chi-square is _____ where _____ refers to the number of categories. In the case where the goodness-of-fit test is used to determine whether data collected from a specific sample can be assumed to represent a population for which the characteristic of interest is normally distributed, the *df* is _____ .

In addition to testing goodness-of-fit, _____ is also used to test whether the way observations are categorized on the basis of one variable influences the way they are categorized on the basis of a second variable. In this case the test is referred to as the χ^2 test of _____ . The formula used to determine the *df* for the test of independence is _____ , where the frequencies are in table format and ___ refers to the number of categories of one variable (number of rows) and ___ refers to the number of categories of the other variable (number of columns).

True-False Items

Place a T for true or an F for false in the space provided before each item.

1. ___ The chi-square statistic is used to evaluate statistical hypotheses when frequency data are collected for different categories.

2. ___ Expected frequency refers to the number of observations that should be obtained based on statements given in the alternative hypotheses.

3. ___ Observed frequencies refers to the actual observations made by an investigator.

4. ___ The formula for χ^2 is $\Sigma[(O - E)/E]$.

5. ___ The goodness-of-fit test is used to determine whether the way observations are categorized on the basis of one variable influences the way they are categorized on the basis of a second variable.

6.____ The null and alternative hypotheses for chi-square are formally stated in relation to the expected frequencies expressed as probabilities, symbolized as *prop*.

7.____ The *df* for the goodness-of-fit test is generally $n - 1$, where *n* refers to the number of observations.

8.____ In forming a decision rule for a goodness-of-fit test of the normality of a distribution, the adjusted degrees of freedom is $k - 3$.

9.____ The test of independence is used to determine if the collected data can be assumed to represent a population for which the characteristic of interest is normally distributed.

10.____ When data are in table format for a test of independence, the degrees of freedom are $(k - 3)$, where *k* refers to the number of categories that are independent.

11.____ A test performed on frequency data to determine whether the way observations are categorized on the basis of one variable influences the way they are categorized on the basis of a second variable is called a test of independence.

12.____ The formula $(r - 1)(c - 1)$ always gives the appropriate *df* for a test of independence.

Multiple-Choice Items

Blacken out the letter corresponding to the correct answer.

1. The symbol *E* refers to
   (a) expected frequency.
   (b) the number of observations that should be obtained on the basis of statements given in H_0.
   (c) a theoretical frequency.
   (d) all of the above.

2. A value for chi-square can be obtained by
   (a) $\Sigma[(O - E)/E]^2$.
   (b) $[\Sigma(O - E)]^2/E$.
   (c) $\Sigma[(O - E)^2/E]$.
   (d) $\Sigma[(O - E]/E]$.

3. Hypothesized population proportions are symbolized
   (a) *O*.
   (b) *E*.
   (c) *prop*.
   (d) *p*.

4. The *df* for the goodness-of-fit test involving hypothesized expected frequencies for one variable is
   (a) $n - 1$.
   (b) $k - 1$.
   (c) $k - 3$.
   (d) $(r - 1)(c - 1)$.

5. A test of independence involves
   (a) two or more categories of a single variable.
   (b) two variables.
   (c) two or more variables.
   (d) a single category.

6. In testing for normality, the *df* for chi-square is
   (a) $n - 1$.
   (b) $k - 1$.
   (c) $k - 3$.
   (d) $(r - 1)(c - 1)$.

7. The formula used to determine the *df* for the test of independence is
   (a) $n - 1$.
   (b) $k - 1$.
   (c) $k - 3$.
   (d) $(r - 1)(c - 1)$.

8. Rejecting H_0 in a test of independence means
   (a) the way observations are categorized on the basis of one variable is contingent on the way they are categorized on the basis of a second variable.
   (b) the way observations are categorized on the basis of one variable is independent of the way they are categorized on the basis of a second variable.
   (c) the way observations are categorized on the basis of one level of a variable is dependent upon the way they are categorized on the basis of another level of the variable.
   (d) none of the above.

9. The actual observations for a defined category made by an investigator are called
   (a) obtained frequencies.
   (b) expected frequencies.
   (c) observed frequencies.
   (d) empirical frequencies.

10. The test used to determine whether sampled category proportions of a population are equal to hypothesized population proportions is called
    (a) a test of independence.
    (b) a two-sample test.
    (c) a goodness-of-fit test.
    (d) a test for normality.

11. In the formula $k - 1$, k refers to the
    (a) number of observations.
    (b) sum of the frequencies.
    (c) number of categories.
    (d) number of variables.

12. In a goodness-of-fit test, rejecting H_0 means
    (a) the fit is a good fit.
    (b) the fit is a poor fit.
    (c) the variables are independent.
    (d) the variables are dependent.

APPLYING STATISTICAL CONCEPTS

Example Applications

1. The chairperson of the psychology department at a small
   liberal arts college was interested in whether or not the
   psychology majors of the past decade chose post-graduate
   vocations that generally agreed with the school's job
   placement statistics for the psychology majors of the
   previous decade. The chairperson asked the job placement
   office to provide general categories for vocations and the
   percentage of students from the previous decade choosing
   those vocations. These are shown in Table 17.1.

   Table 17.1
   Placement Office Percentages (Column 2) of Psychology Majors
   in Vocational Categories (Column 1), Number of Psychology
   Majors of the Past Decade Choosing Those Vocational
   Categories (Column 3), and the Number of Choices per
   Category Expected on the Basis of Previous Percentages
   (Column 4)

(1) Vocational Category	(2) Percentage of Majors	(3) Number of Choices	(4) Expected Choices
Academia	35	62	70
Professional	28	50	56
Managerial	17	48	34
Service Occupations	13	25	26
Clerical	05	10	10
Other	02	05	04

   You should recognize that an answer to the chairperson's
   problem requires an application of **chi-square,** the statistic
   used to evaluate statistical hypotheses when frequency data
   are collected for different categories. You should also be
   aware that the specific test to be applied to this problem

is the **goodness-of-fit test,** the statistical test used to evaluate hypotheses that sampled proportions are equal to hypothesized population proportions. The degrees of freedom for this test is $k - 1$, where k equals the number of categories. The formula used to compute chi-square is $\chi^2 = \Sigma[(O - E)^2/E]$, where E refers to **expected frequency** and O refers to **observed frequency,** the actual observations for the defined category. In Table 17.1 the expected frequency for each category was obtained by taking the category percentage (Column 2) of the total sample size ($N = 200$). For example, the expected frequency of students going into academia are $0.35 \times 200 = 70$. The null hypothesis tested by χ^2 is $H_0: O = E$. The general decision rule is reject H_0 if $\chi^2_{calc} \geq \chi^2_{table}$. For the present problem, $\chi^2 = (62 - 70)^2/70 + (50 - 56)^2/56 + (48 - 34)^2/34 + (25 - 26)^2/26 + (10 - 10)^2/10 + (5 - 4)^2/4 = 7.96$. Since the calculated value of chi-square (7.96) is smaller than the value in Appendix Table 10 (12.59) for $\alpha = 0.05$ and $df = 6$, the decision is to fail to reject H_0. Formally reported, these results indicate that there is no reason to believe that percentages of psychology majors of the past decade choosing the categorized vocations differ from percentages of majors from the previous decade, $\chi^2(6, N = 200) = 7.96$, $p > 0.05$.

2. An educational psychologist was interested in whether the source from which individuals obtain information on current world affairs is dependent or independent of one's level of education. A random sample from each of three education levels (grammar school, high school, college) is selected and the subjects were asked if they got their information on current world affairs from newspaper, television, radio, or other sources. Table 17.2 presents hypothetical observed and expected frequencies.
    Table 17.2
    The Frequency of Individuals at Each Education Level Obtaining Information on Current World Affairs from the Various Source Categories (O) and (in parentheses) Expected Frequencies (E). Marginal (Row and Column) Totals Are Also Shown.

	Grammar School O E	High School O E	College O E	TOTAL
Newspaper	10 (18)	30 (36)	50 (36)	90
Radio	10 (6)	10 (12)	10 (12)	30
Television	20 (21)	50 (42)	35 (42)	105
Other	10 (5)	10 (10)	5 (10)	25
TOTAL	50	100	100	250

You should recognize that this problem also requires use of the **chi-square statistic**, but that it differs from the previous problem in that the test applied is a **test of independence** rather than a goodness-of-fit test. The null hypothesis evaluated by the test of independence is the same as for the test of goodness-of-fit, namely, H_0: $O = E$. The decision rule is also the same as in the previous problem: If $\chi^2_{calc} \geq \chi^2_{table}$, then reject H_0. The df for the test of independence is $(r - 1)(c - 1)$. In our example, $df = (3 - 1)(3 - 1) = 4$. The expected frequencies in Table 17.2 are obtained by multiplying a row marginal total by a column marginal total and dividing the product by the total sample size, which, in this example, is 250. For example, the expected frequency of individuals with a college education obtaining their information from television is $(105 \times 100)/250 = 42$. Chi-square is computed in the usual manner. For this problem, $\chi^2 = (10 - 18)^2/18 + (10 - 6)^2/6 + (20 - 21)^2/21 + (10 - 5)^2/5 + (30 - 36)^2/36 + (10 - 12)^2/12 + (50 - 42)^2/42 + (10 - 10)^2/10 + (50 - 36)^2/36 + (10 - 12)^2/12 + (35 - 42)^2 + (5 - 10)^2/10 = 23.57$. Since this calculated value is greater than the table value (9.49) for $\alpha = 0.05$ and $df = 4$, H_0 is rejected. These results indicate that the source from which individuals obtain information on current world affairs is dependent upon their education level, $\chi^2(4, N = 250) = 23.57$, $p < 0.05$.

Application Exercises

1. In the early 1970's a survey of the American Psychological Association (APA) indicated that the work activity for approximately 39 percent of American psychologists was application/practice, which included such activities as counseling, school psychologist, and psychotherapy. Approximately 18 percent were in research, 24 percent in teaching, and 19 percent in management/administration. A student wanting to know if these percentages hold for today's psychologists sends a questionnaire to 500 psychologists whose names were randomly selected from the APA directory. Of those responding, 150 are in practice/application, 100 are in teaching, 60 are in research, and 90 are in a management/administration position.

    Determine

    a. the test that should be applied in this problem.

    b. the expected frequencies for the four categories.

  c. the degrees of freedom.

  d. a specific decision rule when $\alpha = 0.05$.

  e. the value for χ^2.

  f. whether to reject or fail to reject H_0.

  g. how the results would be formally reported.

2. A social psychologist is interested in determining whether or not a person's political affiliation is dependent on income level. One hundred persons are randomly selected from each of three different income levels (high, medium, low) and are asked whether they are Republican, Democrat, Independent or have some other (including no) political affiliation. For those with a high income level, 60 are Republicans, 20 are Democrats, 10 are Independents, and 10 have other or no political affiliations. The corresponding frequencies for those with a medium level income are 30, 40, 20 and 10. The corresponding frequencies for those in a low income bracket are 25, 50, 10, 15.

Determine

  a. the test that should be applied in this problem.

    b. an organization of data in table format that allows for calculation of expected frequencies for the four categories.

_____

_____

_____

_____

_____

_____

_____

    c. the degrees of freedom.

    d. a specific decision rule when $\alpha = 0.05$.

    e. the value for χ^2.

    f. whether to reject or fail to reject H_0.

    g. how the results would be formally reported.

MEETING THE CHALLENGE OF STATISTICS

The following problems pertain to the memory experiment described in the _Meeting the Challenge of Statistics_ section in

Chapter 1, pages 9-10, of this workbook. The number of syllables or words correctly recalled by the freshmen in each set of experimental and control groups reproduced from Chapter 1 are as follows:

Nonsense Syllables
Experimental: 12, 13, 11, 11, 9, 10, 13, 12, 12, 10
Control: 10, 11, 9, 9, 6, 11, 6, 5, 8, 8

Emotionally Neutral Words
Experimental: 12, 14, 13, 10, 14, 15, 11, 13, 16, 15
Control: 10, 11, 12, 8, 9, 9, 9, 8, 11, 9

Emotion Laden Words (pleasant, **unpleasant)**
Experimental: (9,**6)**, (10,**8)**, (9,**7)**, (8,**8)**, (7,**6)**, (9,**7)**, (10,**6)**, (8,**5)**, (7,**8)**, (9,**9)**
Control: (7,**5)**, (9,**5)**, (6,**5)**, (7,**6)**, (8,**7)**, (7,**7)**, (6,**7)**, (9,**4)**, (6,**5)**, (5,**7)** .

1. Arbitrarily setting a recall score of 11 or above as good recall and 10 or below as poor recall, determine how many experimental subjects had good recall and how many had poor recall. Also determine how many control subjects had good recall and how many had poor recall, putting the results in table format.

2. Determine the test that should be applied in this problem to evaluate whether or not recall is independent of treatment group.

3. Compute the expected frequencies putting them in parentheses in the table in the answer to part *1*.

4. Compute the degrees of freedom.

5. State a specific decision rule when $\alpha = 0.05$.

6. Calculate the value for χ^2.

7. Reach a decision about H_0.

8. State the outcome of the research as you would in a formal research report.

9. On the following page, organize the data of the three experimental groups as a simple frequency distribution and calculate the χ^2 necessary to determine if there is evidence to conclude that the data are collected from a sample where recall scores are not normally distributed in the population of recall scores obtained for subjects allowed immediate sleep.

271

Chapter 17

Workspace for frequency distribution.

10. Determine the degrees of freedom.

11. Determine the decision rule necessary to evaluate H_0 for normality.

12. What should you conclude about the distribution of recall scores of the population of experimentally treated subjects?